D1327269

BLACK MANAGERS

BLACK MANAGERS

The Case of the Banking Industry

By
Edward D. Irons
and
Gilbert W. Moore

Foreword by Phyllis Wallace

PRAEGER SPECIAL STUDIES • PRAEGER SCIENTIFIC

New York • Philadelphia • Eastbourne, UK
Toronto • Hong Kong • Tokyo • Sydney

Library of Congress Cataloging in Publication Data

Irons, Edward D.
    Black managers.

    Bibliography: p.
    1. Afro-American bankers. 2. Banks and banking—
United States—Vocational guidance. I. Moore, Gilbert.
II. Series.
HG1615.7.M5I76 1985   332.1'023'73   84-18304
ISBN 0-03-071938-0 (alk. paper)

Published in 1985 by Praeger Publishers
CBS Educational and Professional Publishing
a Division of CBS Inc.
521 Fifth Avenue, New York, NY 10175 USA

56789 052 98765432

Printed in the United States of America
on acid-free paper

FOREWORD

With the enactment and implementation of anti-discriminatory laws in the mid-1960s, a small cadre of black managers and professionals entered into mainstream commercial banking. Like many of their white peers they were recent graduates from management schools, and expected to enjoy the rewards from success in job performance as they moved up their career ladders. Two decades later, Irons and Moore note that many blacks in banking are frustrated and believe that they have been severely restricted in opportunities for advancement.

Commercial banks are the premier institutions of the financial services industry and hold about one-third of the financial assets of the nation. Significant changes in their operation during the past two decades have been made in response to extensive competition from non-banks and adjusting to a more deregulated environment. Even in such a turbulent environment where many banks have abandoned their conservative and tradition-bound stance, blacks are perceived as interlopers and treated accordingly. Occasionally when all methods of coping with a discriminatory workplace have failed, some blacks have initiated litigation under the Equal Employment Opportunity (EEO) laws.

Commercial banking remains an occupation where sheer talent and hard work will take you only so far. Beyond that the client-banker relationship may be based on a social network and the ability to generate business via this network. Unfortunately, blacks as outsiders to private clubs and elite life-styles have found it very difficult to move into senior management.

For many years banking was an industry in which women workers outnumbered males, more than two to one, but occupational segregation was such that males occupied all of the positions of power and prestige. Even women managers were confined to staff positions. Most of the black male managers and professionals were hired in banking just as a major shift occurred in the utilization of women into well paying and senior positions. Thus, the competition for the best jobs became a zero sum game between black males and white women. Although more black women than black males have been employed in white collar jobs in banking since 1966, the gap between their average salary of $25,630 and $35,000 for black males would appear to more than offset education and prior work experience differences between the groups.

Although the flow (hire rates) of the different race/sex groups have varied significantly over time, it is likely that the present occupational hierarchy (distribution of better paying jobs) follows the same pattern in banking as in other private sector industries — white males, white females, black males, and black females.

The authors of this book conclude that even though racism may be the most pervasive and pernicious factor adversely affecting the careers of blacks in banking, it is in the long term interest of blacks to continue to pursue careers in this industry. Thus, *Black Managers: The Case of the Banking Industry*, can serve many audiences. It is a guidebook for young blacks who may be considering various career options. It can provide survival techniques for blacks in banking who feel isolated in their chosen profession. Most important it may serve as a warning to senior management in banking that there has been a tremendous waste of human resources and that accountability works in two directions.

Well qualified senior black managers have made a psychological contract with their employers to contribute their maximum effort to attain the overall objectives of their banks. The quid pro quo is that the playing field be truly a level one. Senior management has to be held accountable for the manner in which their internal labor markets operate. This case study of the banking industry is not an exception to the rule of how the private sector corporate world has downgraded the effort to bring promising black managers and professionals into mainstream activities.

Phyllis A. Wallace
Professor of Management
Alfred P. Sloan School of Management
Massachusetts Institute of Technology
August 19, 1984

PREFACE

From one perspective this book may be considered an anomaly, one which resulted from a series of fortuitous events. The first such event gave rise to the idea of the book. Two years ago I served as keynote speaker at the annual convention of the National Association of Urban Bankers (minority bankers working in major banks) in Denver, Colorado. On the spur of the moment, I conducted an ad hoc study to ascertain what was happening to the careers of the convention attendees. As it happened this information became the hit of my speech rather than the esoteric stuff that I had prepared relative to the "Impact of the Changing Financial Services Industry on Banking Careers." Since my ad hoc study was not scientific, the attendees asked if I could be persuaded to conduct a scientific study to examine the career dynamics of blacks in the banking industry.

My first reaction was that I am a banking and finance professor, and this subject is not directly finance. It was, however, about careers in financial institutions. More importantly, I had planned to conduct research on an emerging financial instrument that both lenders and borrowers will be using, increasingly, especially if the volatile interest rate environment continues. While I recognized the importance of the "career dynamics" research idea, I was inclined to opt for the financial futures research. As a finance professor, it might provide me more brownie points.

As I was pondering this decision, I received word that one of the sharpest young men that I had been privileged to teach during my 20 or more years of teaching had just been fired after 22 months on the job in a regional money center bank. This was fortuitous event number two. Although this young man had an undergraduate degree in accounting and an MBA in finance, he was fired with the admonition that he could not analyze credits and thus could not develop into a commercial loan officer, a career which he had set his heart on while still in school. Incidentally his father has a Ph.D. in accounting and a CPA as well. He is respected nationally as an accounting educator.

When the young man in question left school, he knew what he wanted out of life and, in my view, had the ability to achieve it.

Unfortunately, as I was to later learn, his career was about to come to a screeching halt, and he couldn't figure out what he had done wrong.

Fortunately, because of my excellent relationship with top management, we were able to get this young man's career back on track. However, this was a traumatic experience for all concerned — the young man, for me, his professor (and unofficial mentor) and perhaps, for the bank.

As I pondered the fate of this young man, I recalled another scenario in which an outstanding female whom I was privileged to teach while she was an undergraduate at Spelman College, finished with honors and went on to complete an MBA in finance at the Wharton School in Pennsylvania. This young lady was so sharp intellectually and in all respects that she literally intimidated both men and women without trying. She was brilliant, attractive, poised, assertive without being offensive, creative and self-assured. She had "success" written all over her when she went into the corporate world.

Her first job was with a major money center bank as a loan officer, her second job with a computer company, and her third job with a new company that unfortunately could not weather the major recession of 1973-75. Within an eight-year period she had moved to her fourth employer.

As I continued to reflect, I recalled that about five years ago, one of our most outstanding male graduates left school with about ten offers. He could have had more but he stopped interviewing. Upon graduation, he accepted a job as a commercial loan officer at a major money center bank. Within three months, he had left the bank. For some reason he did not tell me what had happened. I had to hear it through the grapevine although he knew I wanted to know. He knew that part of my fulfillment was tied up in his success. While no such vote was taken by his fellow students, he probably would have been voted the person most likely to succeed. Only four years has lapsed, and he is on his third job with as many employers, all banks.

As I reflected on the experience of these three young high potential black professionals, it became obvious that each had four things in common:

1. High technical competence;
2. High motivation;

3. Each became frustrated or was fired from his/her early jobs;
4. Each appears to be churning in turmoil in an effort to launch his/her career in corporate America.

These were just outstanding examples. There were others. As I pondered the experiences of these graduates and the research idea that I was being importuned to undertake, what emerged in my mind was this thought: Maybe all of the technical stuff about financial futures, financial spread sheets, or liquidity management etc. are not the most important criteria for success. Maybe, we should take a look at the environment.

The third fortuitous event occurred when a young labor economist came to see me at the request of a highly respected friend. As we sat discussing our respective interests, it became clear that we had a mutual research interest. If I were going to complete the research project within a year, I would need a coauthor. I wrestled with my decision and finally decided I would do it and put Financial Futures on the back burner.

What follows is our effort to examine the environment within which black managers/professionals function in the banking industry. While our data sample was limited to the banking industry, there is considerable evidence that our findings, in large measure, cut across industry lines.

At any rate, having done the research, I feel confident that both my coauthor, Dr. Gilbert Moore, and I will be better professors.

Edward D. Irons

ACKNOWLEDGMENTS

Many people had input into the preparation of this book, either directly or indirectly. Without this assistance, this book would not have been possible.

Perhaps the most significant help came from William Fuller, immediate past president of the National Association of Urban Bankers (NAUB), and vice president of First National Bank of Boston. It was the NAUB, with Bill and his predecessor, Milton Wright, that urged me to conduct the research which resulted in this book. Thanks are in order for the Board of Directors of the NAUB who voted to defray part of the travel expenses associated with the field work phase of the research. In addition, the board encouraged its membership to complete the four-page questionnaire and return it. They also assisted with the arrangement of the personal interview phase of the research. Without this assistance, the research would not have been possible.

We are also grateful to the Research Committee of the Atlanta University Graduate School of Business, who reviewed our research design and awarded us a modest sum toward our travel expenses.

Dr. Phyllis Wallace, professor of management at the Sloan School of Management, the Massachusetts Institute of Technology, brainstormed with me during the conceptualization stage of the research in the early stages and served as a critic of the manuscript. Dr. Arthur M. Jones, the Arthur Vining Davis Professor of Statistics, Morehouse College, Atlanta University, and director of the Morehouse Software Group, assisted by his program associate, Ms. Brenda D. Jones, performed all of the computerized statistical analysis. Dr. Jones also spent many hours with us conceptualizing the various statistical strategies and serving as a critic for selected parts of the manuscript.

Dr. Edward Davis, chairman of the Decision Sciences Department of the Atlanta Graduate School of Business, also criticized selected parts of the manuscript.

Much credit is due Leroy Rankin, editor of the Atlanta University Graduate School of Business Review (AUGSBA) and his editorial graduate assistant Charlene Johnson. Leroy helped us maintain a positive tone when the facts were negative, an invaluable service. He and his assistant read every word of the manuscript.

Thanks are also in order for Mr. James Thompson, director of Financial Aid of Atlanta University for providing us with quality graduate research assistants, of whom Lori Glass, now a banker, and Allen DuBose, now a financial analyst with a major computer company, were outstanding in their research support.

When there were more people in the Business School competing for word processor time than there were hours in the work day, the acting president of Atlanta University, Dr. Kofi Bota, made a word processor available to us in order that we might stay on course with respect to our manuscript submission date.

We are particularly grateful to the 125 bankers in ten major cities who talked in depth with us about their problems and opportunities, their successes and failures, their frustrations and aspirations. These interviews gave body to the statistics which, by themselves can be somewhat sterile.

A special thanks is in order for Ms. Lucy Grisby, chairman of the English Department, Atlanta University, who served as the final editor of the manuscript before it was sent to the publisher.

Last but not least, a hearty thanks is due Lavonia Bess, my secretary/research assistant, who patiently put all of the five or six revisions on the word processor.

To these and others too numerous to name, we are sincerely grateful. In spite of all of the assistance provided by the persons cited above, we accept full responsibility for any errors in the manuscript.

Edward D. Irons
Gilbert Moore

CONTENTS

LIST OF TABLES AND EXHIBITS

TABLES

EXHIBITS

BLACK MANAGERS

1

INTRODUCTION

BACKGROUND

Just two decades ago, blacks and other minorities were literally nonexistent on the managerial or professional level in American industry in general and the banking industry in particular. A confluence of institutional and individual racism, both public and private, had successfully kept blacks and other minorities from participation in this important sector of American life.

Following the great social upheaval in the mid-to-late 1960s, corporate America began, perhaps partially out of conscience, but also as a result of the new legal requirements, to bring minorities into the corporate arena on the technical, professional, and managerial levels.

Before, and concurrent with this newly emerging phenomenon, a number of studies of the hiring and promotion practices of industry with respect to minorities, was conducted. These studies can be loosely divided into two broad classes. The first sought to develop labor market theories that would explain the rationale for the existence of racism and/or discrimination in the labor market. The second class sought to describe the environment created by racism within which blacks and other minority managers functioned in industry and how this environment affected them. Generally no attempt was made to distinguish between the various levels of employees throughout the hierarchy under study, especially management levels, although there were exceptions.

Drawing on labor market theories and statistical models of discrimination at the micro-level, American economists continue to debate the question of the economic status of black Americans. According to one school of thought, the passage of time is healing old wounds, especially since the enactment of Civil Rights legislation prohibiting discrimination in employment. These analysts hold that the labor market status, and whatever differences still exist between blacks and whites are due primarily to the persistence of personal deficiencies among blacks, that is the lack of proper schooling, lack of experience, lack of sufficient motivation, etc.

A less prevalent view traces the labor market difficulties of blacks to structural and systemic economic factors, and finds little evidence to support the conclusion of significant improvement in the status of blacks relative to whites. (Thurow 1975; Ray Marshall 1980; Piore and Doeringer 1972; and Darrity 1982.) Lester Thurow, Michael Piore and Peter Doeringer, for example, are very pessimistic in their assessment of the status and prospects of blacks in the labor force. Regardless of what *individual* human resource managers seek to do, companies, as *institutions*, continue to practice patterns of discriminatory hiring and promotion. Under this scenario, the fault does not rest with the personal difficulties of blacks, but with the existence of internal labor markets, job competition, and discrimination.

David Swinton and others advance the thesis that part of the systemic problem faced by blacks, and to some degree, most Americans, is that they are becoming increasingly over educated and therefore, over qualified, for the jobs they are doing. This phenomenon contributes to under employment, low motivation, and ultimately, low productivity. The irony of this thesis is that it has only been less than two decades that blacks faced the admonition from industry that "We cannot find qualified blacks for the jobs we have."

Each of these views, while based on different and sometimes, conflicting assumptions, nevertheless, provides the reader with some idea of the range of research, attitudes, and conclusions with respect to the status and prospects of blacks in the labor force.

Included among the authors focusing on black managers, the status, the problems of these managers and the environment within which they function are: Glegg and Watson (1982); America and Anderson (1978); Dickens and Dickens (1972); and Fernandez (1975). With the exception of Fernandez, each of the above studies was based solely upon interviews and was written in a reportorial style. That is, their findings are no doubt valid, but it would be difficult for an unbiased researcher to validate their findings independently of the authors.

The additional studies bear some relevance to our study, but are more different than similar. They are: Theibolt (1970) and Alexander (1984).

The Theibolt study focused on employment and credit availability as they relate to minorities. Analyzing both the banking industry in general and minority banking as well, he found extensive discrimination in both jobs and credit with respect to minorities.

The study conducted by Alexander took a different approach. It selected the three largest banks in five money or regional banking centers and sought statistical information regarding employment and credit from the banks themselves. The authors did not concern themselves with minority employees directly. At any rate, this study concluded that women and minorities were severely shortchanged by the banking industry from a statistical point of view. This study, which was originally conducted in 1973 and repeated in 1977, concluded that no measurable change occurred during that interim. Perhaps the study most nearly approaching the analytical model which we utilize in this study was that conducted by Fernandez (1975), entitled *Racism and Sexism in Industry*.

In his study, Fernandez studied the whole spectrum of minorities in one major corporation. He found widespread and systematic discrimination involving all minorities throughout the corporation which he studied.

Given the documented empirical evidence of discrimination in industry in the literature, this study will not seek to replicate that research. Instead, it will seek to definitively describe this environment and the impact that it has upon black managers/professionals in the industry. In the process, we will attempt to ferret out the most significant problems that blacks face in their efforts to build careers in the banking industry. In addition, we will set forth selected strategies for survival/success in that field.

Furthermore, while it seems unlikely that top management does not know what is going on in its respective institutions in this regard, we will proceed under the assumption that executive management may not be aware of what is going on in "the trenches." Accordingly, we will include suggestions which top management may wish to consider, if it is genuinely interested in developing a loyal, highly motivated and productive cadre of black managers and professional bankers. Obviously, if management is aware of the machinations producing the current environment, any such suggestions would be an exercise in futility.

THE BANKING INDUSTRY IN PERSPECTIVE

On a scale of one to ten, in relationship to other industries in the U.S. economic system, the importance of the banking industry would have to merit a ten, in our opinion. The U.S. economy runs on credit; the commercial banks supply the lion's share of short-term credit and a significant amount of intermediate-term credit that fuels the economy. In fact, all (or virtually all) economic activity flows through the commercial banking system. The banker, then, knows who the big guys are and who the little guys are, who has money and who does not, and who the savers and the borrowers are. No other industry is privy to this power-packed information base.

As of 1981, the banking industry employed 1.1 million people, a number which resulted from a compound annual rate of growth of 5.8 percent during the ten-year period ending in 1981. It held total assets of $2.3 trillion by the end of 1982. Significantly, however, the top 100 banks in the United States (less than 1 percent of all the banks) held 44 percent of the industry's assets at the end of 1982. Currently there are approximately 15,500 banks in the United States. It is apparent that there is significant asset concentration in the industry.

If we look beyond the numbers, it becomes obvious that the banking industry can influence the growth, stagnation, or decline of a city or an area, depending upon its decision to provide or withhold credit from that city or area. A creative banker can stimulate the development of an area, while a "passive" one can cause it to drift or deteriorate. The power of the banking industry, therefore, is quite obvious. Given this power, there is little wonder that the banker in any community is perhaps its most respected member.

The current trend of deregulation of the industry is likely to change the way the banking business is conducted and managed, and to decrease the number of banking outlets in the United States.

Nonetheless the lack of significant economies of scale within the industry is likely to cause the demand for well-trained and highly creative bankers to continue at least at the same level as in the last decade, unless of course the economy falters severely.

While the banking industry is as old as our nation itself, it has been less than two decades since black Americans have been afforded the opportunity to become professional bankers. As is true of all organizations, public or private, the management personality of the banking industry sets the tone of the environment within which its employees function. What is the nature and structure of this environment? What impact does this environment have on the careers of black and other minorities? What are the specific forces that influence this environment?

This study, then, seeks to describe those forces from the perspective of the black bankers themselves.

METHODOLOGY

As set forth above, the extensive literature is conclusive that discrimination exists in industry, in general. We, therefore, will not seek to prove discrimination in this industry. Instead, we will attempt to describe the environment from the perspective of those black managers/professionals who are attempting to build careers in this industry.

To accomplish this objective, we compiled three data bases: (1) 16 years of national banking labor sector statistics by race, sex, and job function as compiled by the Equal Employment Opportunity Commission; (2) 300 responses from 1,000 questionnaires sent to black bankers located in 22 states; and (3) personal interviews with approximately 125 bankers in ten geographically representative states.

To understand the trend behavior of the several labor sectors, we both graphed the trend data and computed standard trend analysis. As will be seen later, both the graphs and the quantitative trend analysis produced significant insights into the trend behavior.

As stated, out of approximately 1,000 questionnaires, about 30 percent were returned. The questionnaires were designed to elicit the respondents' perception of their environment as it related to the industry, the specific institution where they worked, the most significant problems which they encountered, the quality of their supervision, the relationship with their peers, the factors governing promotion, and the financial rewards. There were more than 40 variables on the questionnaire that could affect the careers of the respondents. In addition, the instrument elicited a profile from the respondents, including: tenure, function, rank, education, age, size of bank, and sex (see Appendix I).

The sample respondents were divided almost equally between male and female, that is, 52 percent and 48 percent, respectively. More than 40 percent of the respondents held the rank of assistant vice president or above. The average respondent has been in the industry approximately 11 years and at his current bank approximately ten years. More than 70 percent of the respondents had earned a bachelor's or higher degree. Approximately 29 percent had earned MBAs or other masters. Several had Ph.D.s. The average respondent was 33 years old. The banks represented by the respondents ranged in size from less than $1 billion in assets to more than $100 billion with 63 percent above $5 billion. All regions of the United States, covering 22 states, were represented.

With the exception of the profile data, all but two questions were scaled from one to five, with one being excellent or "yes" and five being poor or "no." Our purpose was to gauge the intensity of the feelings of the respondents.

The first level of analysis of the questionnaire was to tally the responses by computer; following this, we reconstructed a "satisfaction index." To accomplish this, we assigned weights from zero to ten to the scales, with five being zero and one being ten. The ten was the highest measure that could be given a question. We then selected the questions that lent themselves to measurement of satisfaction or dissatisfaction, following which, we computed the mean satisfaction index for each question within a category of questions (for example, the industry section) and for the category as a whole. Finally, we computed the composite satisfaction index for all of the categories.

It became obvious early in the research process, both in the questionnaire responses and in the personal interviews, that there is a significant difference between the way the industry treats black males and black females. We, therefore, sought to ferret the cause of this distinction, both quantitatively and qualitatively.

From a quantitative point of view, we dichotomized the labor sector data into two periods; that is, 1966-73 and 1974-81. We then performed a least squares trend analysis for the period 1974-81 and extrapolated the trend to 1990. With respect to the questionnaire, we cross-tabulated the responses by sex and other selected variables.

From a qualitative view, we summarized the personal interviews, which served to give substance to the statistics, thus providing corroboration of the conclusions and examples of how the phenomena under scrutiny actually worked.

LIMITATIONS

This study focuses upon the black managers/professionals in the banking industry, although we did not purposely select blacks to the exclusion of other minorities. Prior research suggests that all minorities face the same problems in industry, varying only in degree. Thus, while we make no hard and fast claim that our findings could be extrapolated to other minority group experiences, there is some evidence that with minor modifications, such extrapolation could be made. Similarly, our focus on managers/professionals does not imply that black employees falling outside these categories are less important in society as the group under scrutiny. In fact, there are a number of studies treating the broader categories of black and other minority employees in industry, and many more are likely in the future.

Our purpose for selecting this category of black employee in the banking industry was to assess the degree to which they are being given opportunities to participate in the decision-making processes that determine what happens to the industry.

It is conceivable that the questionnaire could be a source of certain bias with respect to our conclusions. This could stem from the possible bias from the nonrespondents. There obviously is no way to ascertain the attitudes and experiences of nonrespondents. In this regard, the extreme sensitivity of the information sought by the questionnaire dictated that the instrument be totally anonymous and managed in a strictly confidential manner. Accordingly, respondents were requested to refrain from specifying their names, banks, or cities as a part of the questionnaire. In addition, they were requested to place their questionnaire in an unmarked envelope for its mailing. We were fortunate to have the National Association of Urban Bankers (NAUB) to serve as an intermediary. The national office of NAUB sent out the questionnaires and forwarded the responses to us. This procedure was followed in order to enhance candor from the respondents and to protect their identity. We believe, therefore, that the risk of biased responses has been minimized.

Given the sensitivity of the information in the questionnaire, there was no practical way to conduct a stratified random sample. This would have required positive identification of the respondents *a priori* and would have destroyed the possibility of getting any responses.

In spite of the lack of control of randomness of the sample, we have considerable evidence which suggests that the questionnaire results are a valid representation of the banking environment. Perhaps our most significant validation of the questionnaire was the design and attendant results of the personal interview sample. The personal interview sample was designed to reflect a cross section of bankers, including an equal number of males and females and a pro rata dispersion by rank and tenure. These interviews were arranged by a local member of the club in each of the ten geographically representative cities. In fact, 54 percent of the interviewees were men and 46 percent women. In addition, the average tenure in the industry was 11 years. The average interviewee had been with his current bank for eight years. With respect to rank, 45 percent of the interviewees were at the assistant vice-president level or above, while 47 percent were banking officer or below.

The average age of our interviewees was 34 years. Eighty-six percent of the interviewees had bachelor's degrees or above and 40 percent were MBAs. The average annual salary of our interviewees was $38,000 although there were several above $70,000. Forty-six percent were managers, with the balance being nonmanager professionals.

As with the mail questionnaires, the interviewees were requested not to include their names, banks, or cities in the taped interviews. The questionnaire for the personal interviews covered most of the same basic issues as the mail questionnaire. It differed in that it was open-ended in structure. All interviews were taped and are held in strict confidence by the researchers. When using quotations or examples of problems described by the interviewees, we disguised the interviewees without changing their basic profile, or the substance of the quotation or scenario.

As the evidence shows in the text of the analysis, our interviewee profile compares favorably with the respondents of the mail questionnaire. Perhaps most significantly, the views and perceptions of the interviewees corroborated the responses to the questionnaire.

In view of the above, while there still may be some bias in our responses resulting from the sampling technique dictated by the nature of the data sought, we believe that not only do the views of interviewees and questionnaire respondents represent a valid cross section of black managers/professionals in banking in contemporary America, but also that the findings contained herein will be corroborated in future research.

In our efforts to ascertain the perceptions of the black bankers as they relate to their environment, we purposely confined our inquiries to black bankers, to the exclusion of the "management" of the banks. We are fully aware that we are examining only one side of the equation as it relates to the issues under examination and that the perceptions of the respondents may or may not represent either fact or reality.

As Peter Drucker stated in his work entitled *Management*,

> Perception, we know, is not logic. It is experience. . . . One cannot perceive single specifics. They are always part of a total picture. The "silent language," that is, the gestures, the tone of voice, the environment altogether, not to mention the cultural and social referents, cannot be dissociated from the spoken language.

Whether or not our respondents' perceptions represent the facts, reality, or illusions of the banking environment, does not obviate the fact that these bankers, like all human beings, behave in consonance with their perceptions. To the degree to which their behavior creates problems as a consequence of their perceptions, management must spend time, energy, and money wrestling with these problems. *If, for example, the perceptions of these black bankers are at variance with reality, it is in the enlightened self-interest of management to correct their erroneous perceptions. On the other hand, if their perceptions are in agreement with reality, then management would be wise to seek to address the problems articulated by these bankers.*

Under either condition, the perceptions of our respondents suggest the need for further research focused toward management.

THE ORGANIZATION OF THE BOOK

This book is organized in what we believe to be a rational structure, one that will make it easy for the reader to follow the progression of ideas. We begin with a treatment of the industry, the opportunities and the problems as perceived by our respondents, followed by the respondents' views of the environment within their specific institutions. We next treat specific areas of concern: the quality of supervision, the most significant problems, the promotion criteria and promotion dynamics, the degree to which the respondents have mentors, their relationship with their peers, the stress phenomenon, and the black male-black female different treatment phenomenon. We next include a chapter on "making it" in spite of the environment. The final chapter is directed to management.

2

BANKING: IS THIS THE PLACE TO WORK?

Who does the banking industry attract as employees? What is the job function structure of the banking labor force? How do minorities fit into the labor force of the banking industry? How do minorities perceive the opportunities available to them? What are the most significant problems encountered by black bankers? These and similar questions will be answered in this chapter.

In discussing these issues, we will examine the environment of the industry in general. Then we will examine selected issues as they pertain to the specific institution where the respondents to our inquiries worked.

It should be emphasized that individuals, specific institutions, and specific cities are not identified in this study. We purposely elected to avoid such identification in order to encourage candor on the part of our respondents and to guarantee the confidentiality of their responses. Instead, our study focuses upon patterns of problems and opportunities as they relate to the industry as a whole.

WHO WORKS IN THE BANKING INDUSTRY?

By the end of 1981, 1.1 million people were employed in the banking industry. Of that number, 80 percent were white Americans, while 20 percent were nonwhite. Approximately 12 percent of bank employees were black Americans. As our analysis unfolds, however, it will become dramatically clear that the 12 percent black statistic camouflages a multitude of disparities with regard to the distribution of the job functions within the industry. This report focuses on the black manager/professional labor sector of the banking industry. There is considerable evidence, however, that the treatment of all minorities at all levels by the industry varies only in degree.[1]

By the end of the 16-year period ending in 1981, white males represented 58 percent of all managers in the industry. Significantly, however, this was a 29 percentage point decrease from the percentage of management jobs that white males held in 1966 (see Exhibit

EXHIBIT 2.1
Relative Share of Managers in the Banking Industry, by Race and Sex 1966-1981

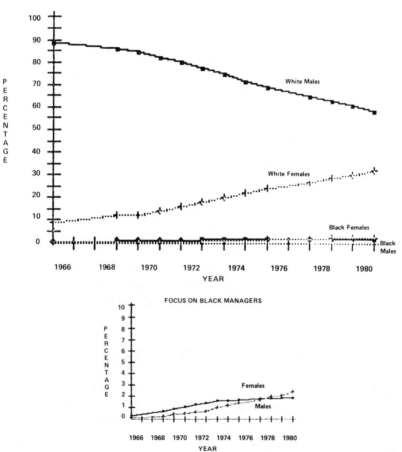

2.1). Black males, on the other hand, represented only 1.9 percent of all management jobs in 1981, an increase of only 1.6 percentage points above their 1966 percentage (Exhibit 2.1).

White women represented 32 percent of the managers in the industry by the end of 1981, an increase of 19 percentage points above their 1966 total. Black women, however, represented only 2.4 percent of the bank management labor force by the end of 1981, an increase of 1.5 percentage points (Exhibit 2.1).

These facts make it obvious that white women are replacing white men at the management level in the banking industry. Much less obvious, however, is the fact that top management in the industry is opting for white women at the expense of blacks, particularly black men, as managers.

BANK EMPLOYEES VIS A VIS
LABOR FORCE PARTICIPATION

One means of gaining some insight into what is happening to various labor sectors in the banking industry is to examine the relationship between the ratio of a particular job function of each sector (that is, race and sex) in the industry, and the labor force participation ratio of that sector.

In this regard, in 1960, 83 percent of all white males were in the labor force. At that time, they held the lion's share or 87 percent of the management jobs in the banking industry. Thus, their management jobs in the banking industry represented 105 percent of their labor force participation level.

By the end of 1981, however, the management jobs held by white males in the banking industry had fallen to 58 percent, while their labor force participation had decreased to 78 percent. This dropped their bank management jobs to 75 percent of their labor force participation.

In stark contrast to white males, 37 percent of white females were in the labor force in 1960. At that time, they represented only 9 percent of the bank management jobs. They, thus, held only 24 percent as many management jobs in the banking industry in relation to their labor force participation. By the end of 1980, white females' share of management jobs had increased dramatically to 32 percent or more than 3½ times the 1960 rate. Predictably, their

EXHIBIT 2.2
Population Ratio by Race and Sex, 1960 and 1980

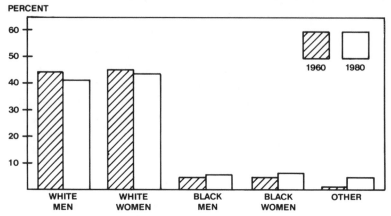

Source: 1980 Census Report, Handbook of Labor Statistics, Aug. 28, 1981.

ratio of bank management jobs to labor force participation increased by a similar amount, that is, to 63 percent.

BLACK AMERICANS AND THE BANKING INDUSTRY – AN OVERVIEW

As for blacks in general, and black men in particular, the evidence is overwhelming that they have been, and continue to be sorely shortchanged by the banking industry.

In 1960, 83 percent of black males were in the labor force. However, they held only *one-third of 1 percent* of the managers' jobs in the banking industry. This represented less than one-half of 1 percent of their labor force participation. By 1980, like white males, but more pronounced, black males had decreased in labor force participation to 72 percent, or by 14 percent, twice that of white males, while their management jobs in the banking industry had increased to *1.9 percent*. Thus, the ratio of their bank management jobs held to labor force participation increased to 3 percent.

In 1960, 48 percent of black females were in the labor force, while their share of bank managers jobs was 2 percent. Their ratio of management jobs to their labor force participation was *4 percent*.

By 1980, the percentage of black females in the labor force had increased to 54 percent, while their share of the banking industry management jobs had increased to 2.4 percent. Thus, their ratio of management jobs in the banking industry to their labor force participation remained unchanged at *4 percent*.

In summary, by the end of 1980, the ratio of management jobs in the banking industry to the rate of labor force participation takes the following order: white males, 75 percent, a significant decrease, but still dominant; white females 63 percent, a dramatic increase; black women, 4 percent and unchanged; and black men at 3 percent, a slight increase. Since the total labor force participation of black males has declined at a significantly greater rate than any other group, the slight increase in black male managers overstates their improvement in the banking industry by the end of 1980.

It should be emphasized here that the management category as defined herein is a grossly ambiguous term. It includes all management activities, whether they involve managing a secretarial pool or functioning as president. To this degree, it is meaningless as a description of what blacks or whites actually do in the industry. Unfortunately, this is the manner in which the Equal Employment Opportunity Commission (E.E.O.C.) in Washington currently requires the data to be submitted. While the term is ambiguous in this context, it applies across the board to all labor sectors. The conclusions derived from this analysis, therefore, remain valid. More definitive conclusions can be derived only at such time as the data are more refined to distinguish between the various levels of management.

PERSONAL INTERVIEW PERSPECTIVES

Significantly, when the statistics regarding the black female were raised with the personal interviewees, there was unanimous agreement among both males and females, that to the degree that black females were in management, with rare exceptions they were in low level operations type jobs, small branch management and staff functions, and not in the commercial lending or investment functions, the heart of the earning centers of banks.

1966-81 – WHO GOT THE JOBS?

Perhaps the most telling evidence of the distribution of jobs in our total economy lies in the participation rates of each sector in the labor force in its share of the increased number of jobs in the economy during the 20-year period ending in 1980. In this regard, of the 52-million member increase in the labor force during this period, white women absorbed almost 25 million, or 50 percent, of the total. White men absorbed slightly more than 16 million, or 30 percent. Black women increased by 2.9 million, or 5.5 percent, of the total. Black men, on the other hand, increased only 1.3 million, or by 2.5 percent. The banking industry follows this pattern (see Exhibit 2.3).

These facts demonstrate that black men are being either systematically excluded or selected out of the labor force in general and, as our study reveals, out of the banking industry, in particular. *By any measure, this is cruel and inhumane treatment of a potentially valuable and productive sector in American society.*

In addition, unless we assume that white males have superior capability in the understanding and execution of sound banking decisions, one could rationally conclude that they still hold a somewhat

EXHIBIT 2.3
Labor Force Participation Ratio by Race and Sex, Percent of the Total Population, 1960 and 1980

PERCENT

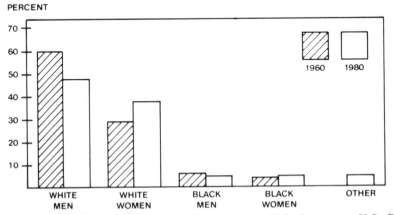

Source: General Population Characteristics U.S. Summary, U.S. Department of Commerce Bureau of the Census, 1980.

disproportionate share of the management jobs in the banking industry in 1981 in relation to the other labor sectors in the industry. Similarly, unless we conclude that white women have the capacity for understanding and making better banking decisions than black men and women, one has to raise the question: What is the criteria for selecting white women managers at a greater rate than black men and women during the period under examination? A similar question would have to be raised with respect to the hiring rate of black women versus black men during the last several years.

Since black men have been relegated to the lowest level of the management hierarchy in the banking industry in recent years, this phenomenon will be the subject of more intensive examination in Chapter 9.

Significantly, the pattern is the same in each of three other broad categories of white collar workers in the industry, that is, professional, technicians, and other (see Exhibits 2.4, 2.5, and 2.6). (For our analysis, we grouped sales workers and clerical workers together in the category termed "other.")

THE SATISFACTION INDEX – THE INDUSTRY

As set forth in Chapter 1, a satisfaction index was computed for questions lending themselves to this analysis. There are two questions which lend themselves to this type of analysis in the industry section.

There is a considerable body of research which suggests that there is a high correlation between productivity and esprit de corps in an organization. Similarly, the degree to which employees are "satisfied" with their working conditions and their associates affects their productivity. Accordingly, our mail questionnaire was designed to elicit our respondents' perception of their environment in the banking industry and to measure their satisfaction level within that environment.

The issues, in general, were couched in the form of a positive statement rather than in the form of a question. We took this approach to avoid the likelihood of a negative bias with respect to the responses. The first statement was: "I believe that banking affords more and varied opportunities for minority Americans than do most [other industries]."

EXHIBIT 2.4
Relative Shares of Professionals in the Banking Industry, by Race and Sex

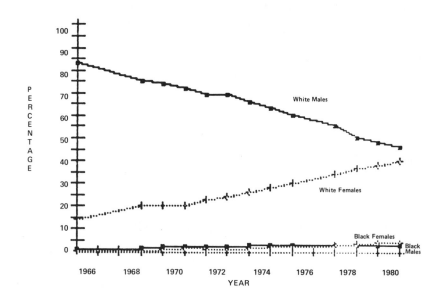

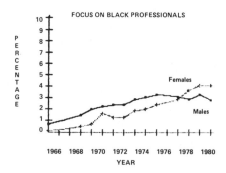

EXHIBIT 2.5
Relative Share of Technicians in the Banking Industry, by Race and Sex, 1966-1981

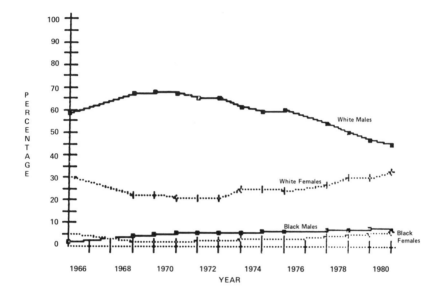

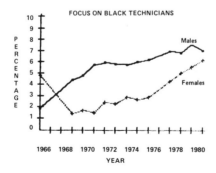

EXHIBIT 2.6
Relative Share of "Other" White Collar Workers in the Banking Industry, by Race and Sex, 1966-1981

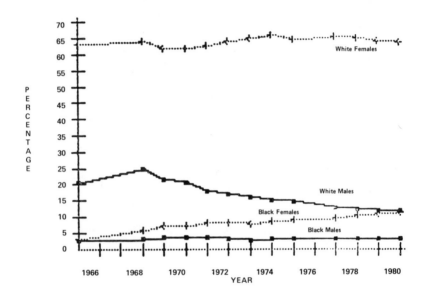

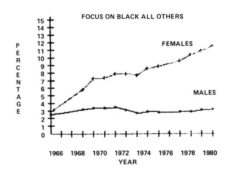

The satisfaction index for this question was only 4.63, suggesting that less than half of the respondents were happy with the opportunities afforded them in the industry. Our respondents are even more negative about their opportunities in the banking industry as they perceive them in relation to their white peers, as evidenced by responses to the second statement: "Minority Americans are currently afforded the same opportunities in the banking industry as white Americans."

The satisfaction index for this question was only 1.94, suggesting that more than 80 percent of the respondents believe that the industry does not provide the same opportunities to blacks as it does to whites (see Exhibit 2.7).

If the perception of these respondents represents reality, one is rationally drawn to one conclusion: *racism*. In addition, the perceptions of our respondents relative to this issue would seem to validate prior statistical research such as that cited in Chapter 1, which concludes that racism is prevalent in industry. In addition, this evidence suggests that industry has yet to heed the admonishment of Robert Townsend, former chief executive officer of Avis Rent-A-Car. In his book, *Up the Organization* in 1965, he said of *racism*:

> Let's face it. The vast majority of corporations are still operating with dice loaded against Jews, black people, and women of all races and creeds.
>
> *Well, it must be clear by now to everybody in touch with reality that it's time to unload the dice.* This has to start with a conviction in the chief executive officer. But if he wants more than a scurry by each division to find a "company black," he had better follow up his bulletin as far down the line as he can and for as long as he is chief executive. Stamping out racism will be a process, not an act, and the chief resistance will be in the personnel office. It is results, not explanations, that count, as in other business action, and you can waste a lot of time just talking.[2]

The personal interviewees were unanimous in their belief that a mentor is necessary if one is to move beyond the lower middle management level in the industry. They were equally unanimous in their perception that "most blacks do not have mentors in the industry." There were exceptions, however. A few black bankers

EXHIBIT 2.7
Satisfaction Index: The Banking Industry in General

1. The Banking Industry affords more opportunities for Minority Americans than most.

2. Minority Americans are given same opportunities as White Americans.

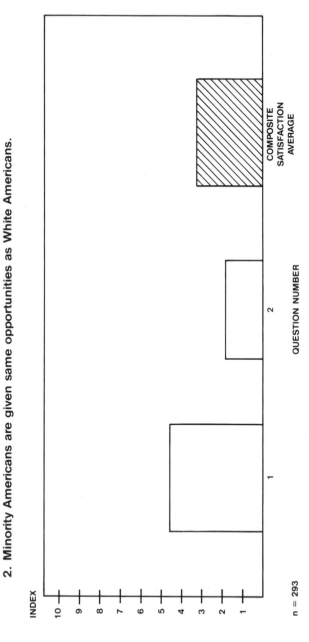

did have mentors. Significantly, there was a distinctly larger number of black women who had mentors than was true of black men.

Those persons who were confident of their mentor relationship exuded self-confidence, high self-images, and tended to rank higher, on average, than those without mentors. This would tend to support the more rapid movement phenomenon of black women versus black men in the industry. The subject of mentors will be treated in more depth in Chapter 5.

THE MOST SIGNIFICANT PROBLEMS FACED BY BLACKS

In an effort to gain insight into the types of problems encountered by blacks in the industry, we devised a question which featured five potential problems and a sixth, labelled "other," which gave the respondent an opportunity to include a problem which, in his opinion, was more important than the ones we had provided. The suggested problems were: racism; not knowing what's going on in the organization; not being given a chance to learn new jobs; poor pay; and the inability to get a mentor.

The number one problem as perceived by the respondents was "not knowing what's going on in the organization." Seventy-five percent of the respondents indicated that this was the most serious problem (see Exhibit 2.8).

The personal interviewees also felt that this was a significant problem. One male banker with ten years of experience cited this example of his inability to find out what was going on:

My complaint is not that I expect my immediate supervisor or manager to be particularly competent. I have never found that to be the case. But beyond that, you are always looking for someone in the institution who might be interested enough to take some time to help you sort out what is going on. Someone who's up there and has a bird's eye view and can say, "I'll tell you what the facts of the matter are." Unfortunately, I don't think black professionals know that many people up there who have that bird's eye view. So it is difficult to find someone who, necessarily, is going to be willing to bring you along.

Obviously, communication networks function on both an informal and a formal basis. In order to know what is going on in

EXHIBIT 2.8
The Most Significant Problems as Perceived by Sample Respondents (Problem Perceived as Number One)

1. Not knowing what's going on in the organization (not in network).
2. Racism.
3. Inability to get a mentor.
4. Not being given a chance to learn new jobs.
5. Poor pay.

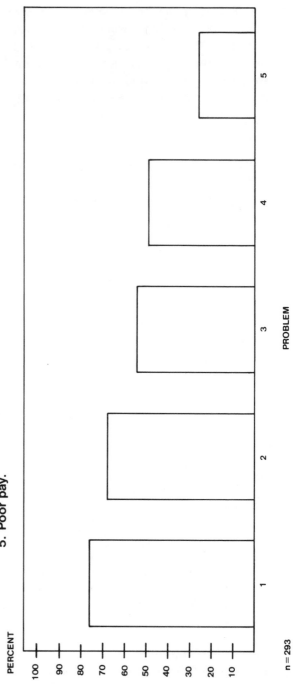

n = 293

the organization, one should be plugged into both levels of the communication process. Unfortunately, our interviewees indicated that, more often than not, black bankers are deliberately kept out of both levels. As an example of how black bankers are kept out of the informal communication network, one highly articulate, well educated, obviously intelligent and assertive young black female banker related this experience:

> If you sit in the room with three of your white counterparts, and you do not own a house, all they talk about is their home, mowing the lawn, shoveling snow, the furnace broke, the plumbing broke, whatever. The minute you own a house, they no longer talk about their house. They will now proceed to talk about their European vacations, or their trip to visit grandma who has retired to Florida. They always talk about things in a way that you will have no input.

The above findings agree with those of John P. Fernandez. He found that 71 percent of black men and 59 percent of black women believed that minority Americans are excluded from informal work groups.[3] In his book, a black woman, first level supervisor, notes: "My peers never invite me to informal discussions, meetings, and luncheons, and many times they discuss issues related to my job." A second level Hispanic woman made these comments: "I am never included. If I were included, it would not be to discuss work related things – probably sex."

These reports suggest that black bankers are inadvertently, or maybe even purposely, kept out of the communication system so necessary to their success, even survival. One canon of sound management suggests that for high productivity management must keep its employees fully informed. Unless employees know what is going on around them, they do not feel that they are part of the team. Thus, they cannot perform to maximum efficiency.

The next most important problem as perceived by the questionnaire respondents was *racism*. The nature of racism is that it is an ambiguous and ubiquitous phenomenon. When it is prevalent, it can pervade all human endeavors involving relationships between the racist and the victim of the racism. It, therefore, could conceivably be the underlying cause of the fact that black bankers are unaware of what is going on around them. In addition, it could rationally be the cause of the other significant problems cited by the respondents, as set forth below. Significantly, racism/sexism was perceived as the most significant problem by 86 percent of the personal interviewees. Those holding this view indicated that while contemporary racism is difficult to prove, because of its covert nature, it is just as pernicious as when it was overt.

When asked to cite examples which led them to the racism conclusion, an articulate 35-year-old black male banker with an MBA from a prestigious business school, ten years of experience, five of which were in banking, described one racist scenario which was commonly used to retard the growth of black bankers:

> If a management job opens up and there is a white male who has done a fair to good technical job in the past, he frequently will be elevated to the job without prior training in supervision. He, therefore, has the opportunity to learn on the job. . . . For black managers, however, they want to make absolutely sure that he can do the job before he is elevated. *They take no risks relative to black bankers.*
>
> To assure themselves that the black manager can do the job, they will often keep him in the lower position often twice as long as their white peers. They will make him accept several laterals without an increase in responsibilities, and maybe after the third lateral, they may say, it looks like he may be ready, but I'm still not sure. So they move him again. Finally if the black banker gets tired moving in circles and leaves, the supervisor says, *"Ah shucks, we were just ready to promote him, . . . if he had just stayed a little longer."*

The third most significant problem cited by the questionnaire respondents was the "inability to get a mentor." The concept of securing and utilizing a mentor has been given great importance in the literature in recent years. It is a generally accepted fact that without a mentor, one is not likely to move beyond lower middle management on the corporate ladder. This concept will be developed in more depth in Chapter 5.

The fourth most important problem was "not being able to learn new jobs." This problem has far reaching implications for the career of black bankers. If one is deprived of the opportunity to learn new skills, one's career is destined to stagnate.

As the chapter on financial rewards will show, black bankers in particular, and bankers in general, earn relatively modest salaries. In spite of this salary situation, the respondents ranked "poor pay" a distant fifth place in order of importance of the most significant problems (Exhibit 2.8). This suggests that pay, after one's basic needs are met, assumes less importance to managers/professionals.

Our research findings compare favorably with the findings of Professor Kenneth Kovak of the University of Maryland in 1976. Kovak conducted a survey in which he submitted a list of ten items to both a worker group and a management group. They were asked to rank these items in order of importance. Significantly, good wages were ranked fifth by the workers, the same as in our findings[4] (see Table 2.1).

Equally significant is the fact that our research revealed that "not being in on things" was the number one problem among our respondents while Kovak's research ranked this factor as the second most important to his respondents. Our conclusions, then, tend to corroborate Professor Kovak's findings[5] (see Exhibit 2.8).

SATISFACTION INDEX – THE BANK WHERE I WORK

After examining the opportunities and problems of the banking industry in general, as perceived by black bankers themselves, it seemed appropriate that we examine the environment of the specific bank where the respondents actually work. While the problems

TABLE 2.1
What People Want from Their Work

	Employee Ranking	*Supervisor Ranking*
Full appreciation of work done	1	8
Feeling of being "in" on things	2	10
Sympathetic help on personal problems	3	9
Job security	4	2
Good wages	5	1
Interesting work	6	5
Promotion and growth within the organization	7	3
Personal loyalty to employees	8	6
Good working conditions	9	4
Tactful disciplining	10	7

Source: Kenneth Kovak, "What People Want from Their Work." *Advance Management Journal* 45 (Spring 1980): 56.

and opportunities of the industry are not separate from those of the particular banks in which the respondents work, there are certain statements which, by their nature, describe the environment of the specific institution more definitively than those directed toward the industry. In this regard, we offered five statements for the reaction of our respondents which were designed to provide insight into the environment of the banks in which the respondents work. The statements were as follows:

1. This company is a good place to work.
2. I am given a chance to do things I do best.
3. I believe I can achieve my career goals in this institution.
4. I would leave the bank if something better came along.
5. My bank is just as vigorously seeking minorities today as they were five years ago.

Considering the five issues as a whole, about half of the respondents are happy with their particular institutions. In fact, on the scale from one to ten, our respondents gave their banks a 5.58 rating regarding the happiness issue (see Exhibit 2.9).

In other words, only slightly more than 56 percent of our respondents indicated that they are happy with their respective banks. One can conclude therefore that the other 44 percent of black bankers are performing their duties under great strain, or quite possibly they are not producing up to their capacity. In either case, their productivity is a function of their environment. It must be emphasized that the environment of any organization is a function of management, beginning at the top.

With regard to the satisfaction index of the individual statements regarding the specific bank, only two of the five items registered positive on the index scale. And, they were only marginally positive. Items No. 1 and No. 2 follow:

1. "This company is a good place to work," with index of 6.1 and,
2. "I am given a chance to do things I do best," with an index of 5.75

It is obviously very difficult for an employee to bring to the work the kind of energy and creativity that results in high productivity if the employee feels only lukewarm about a given institution or situation.

EXHIBIT 2.9
Satisfaction Index: The Bank Where I Work

1. This company is a good place to work.
2. I am given a chance to do things I do best.
3. I can achieve my career goals in this institution.
4. I would leave this bank if something better came along.
5. My bank is just as vigorously seeking minorities today as it was five years ago.

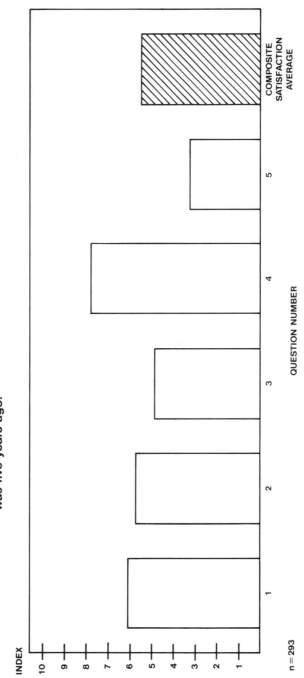

n = 293

Three items in this category are on the negative side of the index. Perhaps the most negative of these was number 4, to which our respondents gave a rating of 7.85. The statement: "I would leave my bank if something better came along," can be interpreted in two ways: the respondents are sufficiently unhappy that either they would leave for the first opportunity that came along, or no matter how happy they are, they would still leave. Therefore, there is either considerable unhappiness with their situations or there is a significant lack of loyalty to the institution. The above circumstance obviously contributes to the cost of recruitment, training, and retention of black bankers, with its attendant turnover implications. While the bankers are still in the employ of their institutions the above environment exerts a downward pressure on their productivity. Under these conditions, neither the bank nor the employee benefits.

This suggests that top management is not giving sufficient commitment and energy to the creation of a positive environment within which black and other minority bankers can grow and develop into loyal and productive managers.

The next most negative statement was number five: "My bank is just as vigorously seeking minorities today as it was five years ago." This statement received a 3.2 satisfaction index. This means that seven out of ten respondents do not believe that their respective institutions are recruiting as vigorously as they did five years ago.

This perception would seem to be borne out by the almost flat growth curve for minority bank employees, especially black men, as seen in the charts cited earlier in this chapter (Exhibits 2.1 through 2.6). Neither does it appear to be a coincidence that this perception of recruitment on the part of the bank happens to be precisely the same index as that given by the respondents to the statement: "I would leave the bank if something better came along." Our questionnaire respondents' perception of this issue was corroborated by the personal interviews. In fact, virtually 100 percent of the interviewees felt that their respective banks no longer vigorously recruited minorities. One female banker in a regional bank expressed the recruitment issue this way:

> Not only are they not recruiting blacks as vigorously as they used to, they are giving those who are here a hard time. When a black employee seeks redress for a particular problem he may be encountering, the

supervisor frequently is likely not only to ignore the problem; instead, he may say something like "He ought to be thankful that he has a job."

THE INDUSTRY'S HIRING-PROMOTION PRIORITIES

In order to get additional insight into our respondents' perception of the current hiring practices of the banking industry as it relates to minorities, we set forth the following statement in the mail questionnaire:

The labor sectors listed below are currently being hired and promoted in the following order in my bank. (Rank from 1 to 4)

| White men | White women |
| Black men | Black women |

Significantly, our respondents ranked the hiring promotion order as follows: White men, white women, black women and last, black men (see Table 2.2).

Equally significant is the fact that without being exposed to the statistics themselves, but rather through observation alone, our respondents are right on target with respect to who gets hired and promoted in the banking industry. From Table 2.2 it can be seen that approximately 70 percent of the respondents thought that white men were the first to get hired and promoted, while 64 percent thought that white women were in second place.

The perceptions regarding the hiring and promotion of black men and women are revealing. Forty-two percent of our respondents felt that black women were in third place while 44 percent thought that black men were in last place with respect to hiring and promotion. If, however, we combine those respondents who thought that black men and women were in third or fourth place, they each total 78 percent.

With respect to our respondents' perceptions regarding white men, one might question their ranking white men first given the rapid upswing of white women in the industry during the last several years. The facts are that while white men have lost position on a

TABLE 2.2
Order in Which Each Labor Sector Is Hired and Promoted

Labor Sector	Rank Order			
	First	*Second*	*Third*	*Fourth*
White men				
Number	207	31	5	3
Percent	(*69.7*)	10.4	1.7	1.0
	(1)			
White women				
Number	35	191	16	4
Percent	11.8	(*64.3*)	5.4	1.3
		(2)		
Black men				
Number	3	11	101	131
Percent	1.0	3.7	34.0	(*44.1*)
				(4)
Black women				
Number	1	13	124	108
Percent	.3	4.3	(*41.8*)	36.4
			(3)	
Not available				
Number	51	51	51	51
Percent	17.2	17.2	17.2	17.2
TOTALS				
Number	297	297	297	297
Percent	100.0	100.0	100.0	100.0

relative basis in the industry they still occupy the lion's share of the "power positions." Similarly, while white women have increased their numbers in the industry on a relative basis during the last decade or so, the facts are that they do not yet occupy the power positions.

The final item in this section sought to ascertain whether or not the respondents felt their career goals were attainable in their banks. This item received a rating slightly below five, which means that it could go either way. In other words, there is a slightly greater chance that one's career goals may not be met at the current bank than there is that they will. Given the response to this statement, there can be little doubt that the respondents would leave their current institutions if something better came along.

NOTES

1. John P. Fernandez, *Racism and Sexism in Corporate Life* (Lexington, Mass.: Lexington Books, 1981), p. 53.

2. Robert Townsend, *Up the Organization* (New York: Knopf, 1970), p. 161.

3. Fernandez, *Racism and Sexism in Corporate Life*, p. 53.

4. Kenneth Kovak, "What People Want from Their Work," *Advance Management Journal* 45 (Spring 1980): p. 56.

5. Ibid., p. 54.

3

MY SUPERVISOR:
SAINT OR DEVIL?

As for the best leaders, the people
do not notice their existence. The
next best, the people honor and
praise.
The next, the people fear; and the
next, the people hate . . .
When the best leader's work is done
the people say,
'We did it ourselves.'[1]

James C. Diggory

THE CRITICAL ROLE OF THE SUPERVISOR

Like it or not, one's immediate supervisor, with rare exceptions,
can make or break an employee's ascent in an organization. Not
only do most employees not have the opportunity to select their
bosses, they also do not have control over the type persons they
may be.

The inherent power of the supervisor coupled with the various
management styles and types of persons that may occupy the position of supervisor dictate that the wise employee have two important characteristics: flexibility and patience. Without these two
qualities, our research suggests, an employee's future can be derailed,
perhaps even destroyed.

If one is fortunate enough to inherit a "good boss" (and our respondents reveal that it is indeed fortunate when one does), one need not be concerned with the problems encountered if one inherits an SOB as a boss, at least for as long as the privilege of having the good one lasts. Unfortunately, because the nature of organizational behavior is change, even those who at times have good bosses may at other times wind up with intolerable ones. It seems to us, therefore, that it might be instructive to our readers to set forth here the role, some of the leadership styles, and the types of persons one might inherit as a boss. In addition, we will suggest behavior patterns that may assist employees both to learn from and endure the intolerable boss, at least until they get reassigned to another SOB, a different type, that is.

The roles of supervisor and worker are interlocked in such a way that there is always the opportunity for the self-esteem of both to increase, not merely while the work gets done, but precisely because it is getting done. The higher the level of the supervisor, the greater the responsibility for setting the tone of the organization. The quality of supervision or administrative activity creates the atmosphere which tells everyone else in the organization what "getting ahead" means. *It determines whether solid, honest, generally useful abilities, or merely status-getting abilities are important.* Within an organization this effect is transmitted more rapidly than a contagious disease in an epidemic and its effects are more far-reaching and lasting, whether they be for good or ill.[2]

LEADERSHIP STYLES AND PERSONALITIES

No two supervisors are likely to be alike either in personality or in leadership style. Supervisors are likely to vary in leadership style along a continuum from one who involves himself in great detail in the total operation of the organization, to one who abhors detail and leaves most of it to subordinates. This type may delegate little authority and responsibility, thus holding the reins very tight, or may delegate most of the work. This type of supervisor may transmit much information as to what is going on in the total organization, or may withhold much information. A supervisor may be technically oriented or a generalist, leaving the technical details to subordinates. Some supervisors prefer to have in writing all the information submitted to them by subordinates; others eschew memoranda, preferring the use of oral communication systems. Some supervisors work long hours; others go home at the close of business. Some supervisors like to hold regular and extensive meetings; others hold few meetings. Supervisors may be competent or incompetent, experienced or inexperienced.

Whatever personality or leadership style the supervisor possesses, it is the responsibility of the subordinate to adapt and manage the relationship to his own benefit. *It is a serious error to assume a passive approach to the relationship between you and your boss.* In fact, in the words of Gabarro and Kotter, the subordinate has to *manage his boss*.[3] At a minimum, the subordinate needs to appreciate the boss's goals and pressures, and strengths and weaknesses. He needs to be aware of the boss's organizational and personal goals if he is to successfully manage the relationship.[4]

INTOLERABLE BOSSES: A CLASSIFICATION BY BEHAVIOR

All bosses, unfortunately, are not good bosses. In fact, many bosses are given special names by their employees, such as the rear of a donkey. But what are the characteristics of bosses that make one dislike them? If one accepts the fact that supervisors are a cross section of society, then it is hardly surprising that they are likely to possess the same distribution of strengths and weaknesses that are found in the larger society. Obviously, we have everything in society from saints to crooks. One would have to be suffering an illusion to think that supervisors would be different.

Poor supervisors have been classified in various ways by different authors. Perhaps the most novel and comprehensive classification we encountered in our research was that advanced by Michael M. Lombardo, Project Manager and Behavioral Scientist at the Center for Creative Leadership in North Carolina, and W. McCall, Jr., Director of Research at the center.[5] Both have spent nine years studying leadership and management in complex organizations.

They derived their classifications from interviews with 73 highly successful executives in three large industrial corporations. These 73 executives were asked about their experience with intolerable bosses. From the responses, Lombardo and McCall synthesized the experiences of these executives into ten classes of supervisor types. They dubbed the ten classes Rogues Gallery (see Exhibit 3.1 for

EXHIBIT 3.1
Rogues Gallery

Snakes-in-the-Grass: The most frequently mentioned failing in our catalogue of bossy sins is lack of integrity. These men lie, fail to keep their word, employ their authority to extort confidential information and then use it to a subordinate's disadvantage and just generally can't be trusted.

Attilas: The dictators, little Napoleons or martinets, as they were also called by our executives, are not dismayed by a string of mistakes, and take offense if anyone else makes decisions or stands out in any way. They are at once the easiest to spot of the intolerable types and the hardest to cope with; they simply sit on people.

Heel-Grinders: "They treat others like dirt," one man said. They belittle, humiliate, and demean those beneath them, showing their insensitivity in many ways. One popular sport: "raking people over the coals in front of a group."

Egotists: These blowhards know everything, won't listen, and parade their pomposity proudly. One boss we heard about plays a ruthless game in which he brings up a seemingly insurmountable problem and then disparages every solution proposed. When his subordinates run out of ideas, he presents them with the solution he had in mind all along.

Dodgers: These bosses are the antitheses of egotists. They are unable to make decisions and shirk responsibilities whenever possible. They have never heard of the saying, "Lead, follow, or get the hell out of the way."

Incompetents: The men in this group don't know what they are doing and won't admit it. They are prime examples of the Peter Principle, men who have risen to the level of their incompetence.

Detail Drones: They go strictly by the book, delight in detail – the pettier the better – and love to make big issues out of little ones.

Rodneys: For reasons that sometimes aren't clear, Rodneys just don't get any respect from anybody around them: subordinates, bosses, or strangers in the street.

Slobs: Their personal habits, appearance, or prejudices are intolerable to others. One described to us is a drunk; another sleeps on the job.

Miscellanies: There are a few cases in which the boss doesn't seem especially villainous, but some personality clash or poor chemistry between boss and subordinate causes problems the latter can never overcome.

Source: Michael M. Lombardo and Morgan V. McCall, Jr., "The Intolerable Boss," *Psychology Today* (January 1984): p. 46.

explanation). The classes were as follows: snakes-in-the-grass, attilas, heel-grinders, egotists, dodgers, incompetents, detail drones, rodneys, slobs, and miscellanies.

It may be somewhat unsettling to the reader, as it was to us, to learn, as did Lombardo and McCall, that the most frequently mentioned failing in their catalogue of "bossy sins" was a lack of integrity. These men lie, fail to keep their word, employ their authority to extort confidential information and then use it to a subordinate's disadvantage, and just generally cannot be trusted. This is the description of the "Snake-in-the-Grass" boss.

We believe that the Lombardo-McCall Rogues Gallery is sufficiently profound that the reader would do well to study and reflect upon this description of the types of intolerable bosses for which one may find oneself working. At least, what the 73 successful executives studied proved is that one can succeed in spite of the impediments of an intolerable boss.

While the characterization of intolerable corporate managers by Lombardo and McCall may border on the cynical, their findings tend to agree with those of Dr. Michael Maccoby, a Fellow in the Institute for Policy Studies and Director of the Harvard Project on Technology, Work and Character. In his book on *New Corporate Leaders*, Maccoby concluded that:

> Given our socioeconomic system with its stimulation of greed, its orientation to control and predictability, its valuation of power and prestige above justice and creative human development, these [behavior patterns] may be as good as we can expect from corporate leaders.[6]

WORKING WITH AN INTOLERABLE BOSS

The Lombardo-McCall study shows that armed with an understanding of "where the boss is coming from," an employee can work out an appropriate strategy for working with him with a minimum of frustration until he or his boss changes positions. These successful executives also learned several other lessons that all who may travel the same paths may wish to consider. They are as follows:

1. It is a rare occasion when one can win an open confrontation with a boss. Best course of action, do not try.

2. It is a certainty that the employee or the boss will be changed in the predictable future; thus, the situation is temporary. (Wait it out.)
3. One is not likely to change the boss. Best bet, try changing oneself.
4. One can learn how to disagree without destroying the relationship.
5. One can learn how to manage correctly by watching how to manage incorrectly.
6. One can learn how to treat subordinates by experiencing how they should not be treated.
7. One can learn how to cope with adversity.
8. One should look on the experience as a learning experience, and learn.
9. If one has exhausted all emotional and creative resources without relief, one should leave the job.
10. If leaving the job is not financially feasible at the time, one should keep his head low until he can leave.[7]

Since it is a certainty that every employee is likely to encounter an intolerable boss at some point in his career, the above lessons may be of some value in keeping one's career on track.

Obviously there are exceptions to any rule. In fact, we encountered such exceptions in the interview segment of our research. A select few of our personal interviewees were able to successfully circumvent the immediate supervisor in their efforts to ameliorate their problems. In these cases, the employee either took a calculated risk and won or had a mentor on whom to rely to protect his flank. These were exceptions, however, and should be judged in that context.

TECHNIQUES OF CIRCUMVENTING
AN INTOLERABLE BOSS

With respect to risk taking, the interviewees repeatedly emphasized that one must be a risk taker to move up the corporate ladder, or even to sustain one's present position. Those who sit back and wait for problems to solve themselves and for opportunities to come their way are more than likely to be left frustrated or passed by. Taking calculated risks should be distinguished from gambling. Prudent risk taking requires an assessment of all of the available facts, the potential gain and potential loss, and making a judgment as to the chances of winning. In a situation such as this, when the stakes are high, it is generally advisable to test one's judgment on a trusted advisor or friend. The chances are virtually 100 percent that the problem is not unique. Many people have faced this problem. Why, then, should one go through the process of "inventing the wheel," when the wheel has been around for generations?

Gambling, on the other hand, overlooks the risk/gain assessment. The gambler plunges ahead, more often than not, and frequently finds out too late that the risks outweighed the gains and in the process discovers that his career is either stifled or destroyed. Those interviewees who successfully circumvented their rough bosses were always careful to consult with their mentor or other advisor *before* taking a risk that could backfire.

These bankers emphasized that for best results, before problems present themselves, one should be constantly on the alert for opportunities to get one's name out into the organization beyond the immediate supervisor. This can be legitimately done by sending copies of achievement memoranda, relevant letters, and reports to persons of "power" in the normal course of doing one's job.

One banker who had successfully circumvented her rough boss, stated that:

> I make it my business to attend all meetings, social events and other gatherings that will put me in contact with persons of power *beyond* my immediate department. I want them to know me by name. You would be amazed how important it is for them to know your name, it is no accident that when they begin looking for someone to fill a slot, your name is likely to emerge among the prospects.

Obviously, one has to handle these relationships prudently and judiciously. If they are handled well, these contacts can be a great source of strength as one seeks to keep his present job, to transfer, or to move up the ladder.

MY SUPERVISOR – AN INTRODUCTION

Because the supervisor plays such a critical role in the career development process of an employee, we deemed it important to measure the quality of the supervision of the banking industry as perceived by black bankers. We, therefore, devised seven questions from which we could compute a satisfaction index as a part of the mail questionnaire. The questions were designed to provide us with some insight into the quality of supervision which influences the careers of black bankers.

SATISFACTION INDEX – MY SUPERVISOR

Taken as a whole, the respondents to our mail questionnaire gave their supervisors an average rating: (5.5) – not good, but not bad either. There were seven questions in the section on supervision. The indexes for them ranged from a low of 3.8 to a high of 6.9. Two of the questions were below five on the scale, while five were slightly above five (see Exhibit 3.2).

On the negative side of the index, the lowest rating was given to the statement: "My supervisor invites me to social functions outside the bank." Our sample respondents gave this statement a 3.8 rating, suggesting that more than six out of ten say that their supervisors do not invite them to social functions outside the bank. Obviously, social functions outside the bank organization are the private province of all employees of any organization, from the president down, and it is hard to conceive of a circumstance in which such activities should be viewed in any other context. Social functions are designed for people to relax with and enjoy their friends and acquaintances.

However, there has been considerable research regarding organizational behavior which concludes that there is a high correlation between productivity and *esprit de corps*. Esprit de corps is most effectively cultivated through social interaction.

If a high level of esprit de corps is an important characteristic of a highly productive organization, one would have to raise the question: Why would the banking industry exclude such a significant portion of its managers/professionals from this loyalty/productivity building process? A further question might also be relevant: Is this exclusion deliberate or inadvertent? In either case, the net effect is the same.

Given the social mores of this country, with respect to black/white social interaction at this point in history, it is not surprising

EXHIBIT 3.2
Satisfaction Index: Quality of Supervision

1. My supervisor is competent in doing his/her job.
2. My responsibilities are clearly defined.
3. My supervisor is concerned about my welfare.
4. My supervisor helps prepare me for the next step on the career ladder.
5. My supervisor gives me credit for my ideas.
6. My supervisor invites me to social functions outside the bank.
7. My performance evaluations are fair and objective.

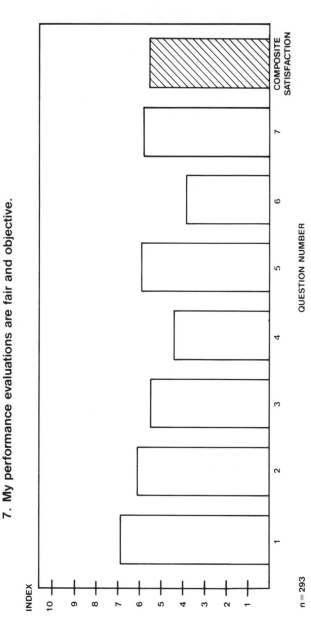

42

that there is almost no genuine social interaction between white and black employees in the banking industry. Nonetheless, for those institutions which want to build the highest level of loyalty and productivity for the competitive times ahead, it would seem to be in their enlightened self-interest to adapt an "outreach" approach to their black managers and begin to include them more in their social dynamics. Those who do, in our opinion, will find that, as was realized in professional basketball, there are potential "Dr. J's" all around them just waiting to be discovered. And when they are, they are likely to become good "profit centers" for the bank, just as the real Dr. J. is for basketball.

The second most negative satisfaction index was statement number 4: "My supervisor helps prepare me for the next step on the career ladder." Our sample respondents gave this statement a 4.3 rating, suggesting that almost six out of ten respondents indicated that their supervisors do not prepare them for their next step up the ladder.

This conclusion was corroborated by our personal interviews. In fact, a majority of the interviewees felt that this was a major problem. As stated by a Midwestern banker with an MBA and ten years of experience:

> . . . There is no real career guidance. . . . I can recall one particular incident at my previous bank where a white male applicant came into the bank to apply for a job. It so happened that he was dressed inappropriately. However, he had gone to a particular school where the CEO and other senior officers at the bank had attended. So rather than turn this guy away, they sat the guy down and explained the dress code to him. "This is what we expect." In a week or two he was hired.
>
> On the other hand, the average black who would have encountered the same problem would have been turned away. . . . Take it a step further, for white employees, there is constant appraisal and recommendations that would certainly insure a high probability of success for them. I would like to refer to this as programmed to fail or programmed to succeed. I think we [blacks] are more programmed to fail.

As will be seen in a later chapter, dress is a very important criterion for success in the banking industry. The above scenario illustrates a lack of positive support which blacks encounter in their career pursuits. They also frequently encounter both overt and covert behavior from their supervisors which exerts a downward pressure on their career aspirations. A Southeastern banker with seven years of experience cited such an example:

> There was an individual who was right in the crest of his career, and there was a loan situation. Going in, it was a prudent loan decision. Coming out, it was a negative decision. That is not unusual. All loan officers sometimes make bad loans. That individual was in the career review process being reviewed on an annual basis. It happened, though, that this individual was black and the borrower was black. There was a $50,000 charge-off. As a result, that one particular charge-off had a direct impact on his performance review. That individual had been performing *above average* and *commendable* for his entire banking career. When it came down to that one particular incident, when the performance review was given, he was given a commendable minus; however, when that individual asked for a signed copy of the performance review, the rating was changed. The individual went to a senior management person regarding this issue who told him: "I know it's unfair but there's nothing that can be done."

What this scenario suggests is that upper management supports lower management where blacks are concerned even when lower management is wrong.

This is a serious indictment of the supervisory personnel in the banking industry. What this does is to place upon the shoulders of the black employee the total responsibility of growth. This has both a frustrating and a stifling effect upon those employees who are managed in this manner. If these employees are expected to grow and become productive employees of the industry, they must be given career path alternatives and guidance as to how these objectives can be achieved.

HOW SOME INDUSTRIES DO IT – AN EMPIRICAL REVIEW

In this regard, the banking industry might wish to take a page from some other industries. Exxon Oil U.S.A., for example, includes in the evaluation criteria of all of its managers an assessment of the degree to which each manager is training each of his employees for the next step up the ladder, including a person who could do his job.

This system prevents an arbitrary supervisor from stifling or destroying the career of a potentially productive employee. It systematizes the human resource development process to the mutual benefit of the individual employee and the corporation. It is conceivable that the banking industry is following the Exxon (or similar) model. However, if it is, it is excluding its black managers from the process.

As stated earlier, there were five questions to which the respondents gave their supervisors a marginally above average rating. These questions had to do with the competency of the supervisor: "whether or not he defined the employee's duties," "whether or not the supervisor was concerned with the employee's welfare," "whether or not the supervisor gave the employee credit for his ideas," and "whether or not the evaluations were fair" (see Exhibit 3.2).

Although the composite average of the satisfaction indexes of the above questions was marginally above average, suggesting that the supervisors were neither excellent nor poor, additional insights may be gleaned by examining the extremes of the rating scales.

With respect to the competency of the supervisor, only 12 percent of the respondents rated their supervisor "excellent"; this was only marginally higher than the number feeling that their supervisor was "poor," 9 percent. With respect to the other supervisory factors, there were also only marginal differences between excellent and poor in the ranking. With respect to the two negative factors, that is, whether or not the supervisor helped prepare the employee for the next step up the ladder and whether or not the supervisor invited the employee to social functions, it logically follows that the responses would be heavily weighted toward the negative end of the scale, since the index itself was negative. In this regard, three times as many respondents thought the supervisor was "poor" relative to the "concern for welfare" issue than thought he was "excellent." Similarly, almost four times as many respondents rated the supervisor "poor" as those who rated him "excellent" with respect to the "social function" issue.

Clearly, these two issues are basic to the ultimate success of most employees. The perception that the supervisor does not help prepare the employee for the next step on the career ladder is likely to stifle the employee. If the banking industry utilized the practice of selected other well run industries, these supervisors would be downgraded for their negligence in this responsibility.

Similarly, since the social function is such an integral part of most business structures and is the key to "knowing what is going on," supervisors who exclude selected employees from this process deprive them of an important component of the communication system. Not knowing what is going on not only has a stifling effect upon the career of the employee, but it also inhibits his efficiency. No employee can be expected to give his best in an environment within which he does not know what is happening.

INTERVIEWEE EXPERIENCE

The questionnaire responses to the supervisory issue were in general corroborated by the personal interviews. The interviewees had worked for both good and bad supervisors. However, those who had worked for good ones were in the minority.

Perhaps the most frequently mentioned problem was "that the supervisors frequently would not provide either guidance in the present responsibilities, or the kind of feedback that an employee needs to determine how he is faring." A number of the interviewees indicated that they had to "insist with persistence" on a written evaluation of their performance. Even then, the evaluation was grudging and frequently vague. The impact upon the employee under these conditions is obvious; it creates a feeling of uncertainty within him.

In addition, many interviewees indicated that their supervisor did not share information with them as to what was going on within the organization in general. Frequently, when the employee realized that some important event was occurring, it was too late for him to benefit from it. His white peers, however, seemed always to know when something "good is coming down the pike" in sufficient time to avail themselves of possible opportunities. The practice of withholding information from black employees obviously contributes to the "snail paced" upward mobility of black bankers in the industry.

NOTES

1. James C. Diggory, "Status, Ability and Self Esteem," *Frontier of Management Psychology*, ed. John C. Diggory (New York: Harper & Row, 1964), p. 125.

2. John G. Gabarro and John P. Ketter, "Managing Your Boss," *Harvard Business Review* 58 (January-February 1980): pp. 94-95.

3. Diggory, "Status, Ability and Self Esteem," p. 95.

4. Michael M. Lombardo and Morgan V. McCall, Jr., "The Intolerable Boss," *Psychology Today* 18 (January 1984): pp. 44-47.

5. Ibid., p. 45.

6. Ibid., p. 46.

7. Ibid.

4

HOW DOES ONE
GET PROMOTED
AROUND HERE?

> There are few more crucial issues in
> our society than . . . who gets pro-
> moted and why.[1]
>
> Gorda W. Bowman

To be respected for one's worth and to be promoted as a consequence of that respect is one of the highest aspirations of the American worker.

Promotions are clearly one of the most important criteria that
a supervisor has at his discretion with which to motivate employees.
The manner in which this important management tool is used can
determine the level of motivation, not only as it relates to an individual, or a segment within an organization, but also to the total
organization. In the final analysis, it is the responsibility of the
supervisor to motivate the employee. It also is axiomatic that the
productivity of an employee, or of an organization, is directly
related to the degree of motivation of the employees within that
organization.

In this chapter, we will examine the promotion process that
is operational in the banking industry as it is perceived by our
respondents. We will also examine both the criteria and the dynamic
which undergird this process.

INDUSTRY PROMOTION CRITERIA

If one is to find his way up the industry ladder, one has to understand what the criteria for promotion are. In an effort to get some insight into black bankers' perception of the criteria for promotion, we listed seven criteria in our mail questionnaire and asked the respondents to rank their importance on a scale from one to five, with one being very important and five being totally unimportant.

The seven criteria were: technical knowledge, communication skills, personality, office politics, hard work, appearance, and education. Education and communication skills had two subheadings each, bringing the total number of criteria to 11.

"Work hard and keep your nose clean and your chance will surely come" is the wisdom that is widely dispensed in the black community from childhood. We, therefore, expected this criterion to be number one, or close to it, on the list of promotion criteria. We were somewhat surprised, however, that not only did it not come in first, it did not come in second, third, or fourth, in the perception of the respondents. In fact, it came a distant eighth in order of importance. Only 15 percent of the respondents felt that hard work was the most important criterion for promotion, while 44 percent felt that it was ranked one or two on the scale of importance.

Before discussing the number one criterion for promotion as perceived by our respondents, we feel compelled to reveal the source of an additional surprise. Like hard work, we thought that education would be considered in the top two or three most important promotion criteria. Instead, education was rated number ten in order of importance, in spite of the fact that 70 percent of the respondents were college graduates. Approximately 11 percent of the respondents felt that education was the most important criterion for promotion, while approximately 39 percent ranked it number one or two on the scale. Similarly, the value of an MBA came in ninth and the school from which one graduated came eleventh, or last.

It should be emphasized here that although hard work and education were ranked relatively low on the promotion ladder criteria, this should not be interpreted to mean that they are, in fact, unimportant. This fact was clarified in our personal interviews. The most common explanation of the low ranking of education among the interviewees was "Education is only important as a means of entry into the banking system. Once one gets in, the criteria changes from education to productivity. If one can't produce, it doesn't matter how much or where he acquired his education; he is not likely to make much progress." With respect to hard work, the interviewees indicated that "hard work is a given." Everybody who expects to get promoted works hard. Therefore, hard work is neutralized and is given relatively little consideration in relation to other promotion criteria.

In summary, *one is not likely to get into the system without appropriate education; but having gotten in, if he does not produce, his education will not sustain him. Similarly, hard work by itself will not get one promoted, that is, at the management/professional level. Without hard work, however, one is not likely to get promoted, either.*

PROMOTION DYNAMICS

In general, the personal interviews not only corroborated the questionnaire responses but also cited specific examples of how the criterion worked. In this regard, virtually 100 percent of the interviewees indicated that the most important criterion for promotion was "who you know," or "being plugged into the political system." Perhaps the most poignant criterion cited by both males and females, and not infrequently, was "kissing ass." This characterization of this phenomenon was variously referred to as "brown nosing," "toming," "kissing up," and "doing everything one possibly can both oficially and personally to make one's immediate supervisor look and feel good."

As an example, one female banker related a story about how her fellow employees behaved when their female boss had a baby: "They fawned over her, gave her presents and generally just went overboard to show their affection for her."

Ironically, the criterion that we thought would come at the top came in at or near the bottom while the one we thought would come in at or near the bottom of the scale of importance came in at the top. The number one criterion for promotion as perceived by our respondents was "who you know, or office politics." Seventy-one percent of the respondents thought that this criterion was either the most important or next to the most important (see Table 4.1).

Of the five questions that lent themselves to satisfaction measurement, one was deemed to be ambiguous and was eliminated. The satisfaction index of the remaining four questions was considerably below average, or only 3.7. This suggests that more than six out of ten respondents were less than happy with the promotion dynamics of their respective institutions (see Exhibit 4.1). Of the four questions dealing with promotion dynamics, only the one dealing with "my chances of promotion" was average or above. And it was only marginally above average, or 5.2. The other three questions were each below average with respect to the index.

Falling at the bottom of the index spectrum on this issue was the question that sought to compare the chances of promotion of minority Americans with that of white Americans. The index for this question was 2.27, which suggests that almost eight out of ten black bankers believe that their chances of promotion are not as good as that of their white peers. Such a perception cannot help but exert a downward impact upon the motivation and loyalty of black and other minority employees. This conclusion tends to follow logically from information presented in the industry section

TABLE 4.1
Promotion Criteria

| Criteria | *Ratings* | | |
	1	*2*	*Total*
Who you know (office politics)	38.3	32.6	71.0
Communication skills – in general	21.5	38.3	59.8
Communication skills – oral	19.0	41.4	61.0
Personality	21.1	36.4	57.5
Appearance	16.1	41.0	57.1
Communication skills – written	18.0	34.1	52.1
Technical knowledge	15.7	31.8	47.5
Hard work	14.9	29.1	44.0
Education: an MBA	12.3	28.7	41.0
Education: in general	10.7	28.4	39.1
Education: your school	9.6	26.4	36.0

EXHIBIT 4.1
Satisfaction Index: Promotion Dynamics

1. Promotions are handled fairly in this bank.
2. My chances for promotion are good.
3. Minority Americans have the same chances as White Americans.
4. I have a mentor.

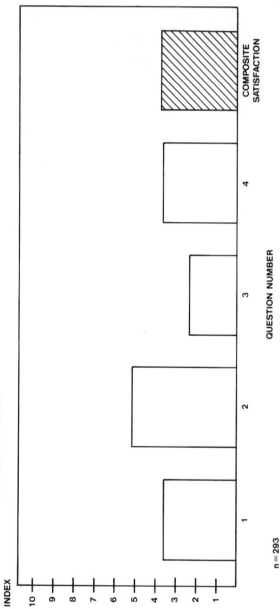

of Chapter 2, in which eight of ten black bankers indicated that they would leave the bank if something better came along. As shown in Chapter 2, equally low on the satisfaction index, falling at about the same level, were the two questions dealing with the fairness with which promotions are handled and whether or not black bankers have mentors. The satisfaction index for these two questions was 3.64 and 3.68, respectively. Thus, six out of ten respondents do not have mentors, and they do not believe that the promotion system is handled fairly (Exhibit 4.1).

INTERVIEWEE EXPERIENCE

The personal interviews corroborated the views of the mail questionnaire with respect to the promotion and fairness issue. Commenting on the way the promotion system regarding blacks works in his bank, a male loan officer with ten years' experience in a regional bank, said:

> In order for a black to succeed in this bank, he has to be aware of who knows who and how comfortable they are with you. It's unlike any other place I've ever been, that is, city-wise. Unless a black comes 360 degrees full circle and bends over backwards to prostitute other blacks and minorities to their satisfaction, they're not going to feel comfortable with you. In other words, you have to do the things that they would like to see. You have to make them aware that you are in total allegiance to and with them and against other blacks. That's the way it works in this bank.

The above statement appears strange. As strange as it seems, we repeatedly encountered this phenomenon in our personal interviews. Some interviewees referred to it as the "hour-glass mentality," with respect to blacks.

As another interviewee put it: "They will only let a few blacks through the system, but before they let you in, they want to make sure that you aren't hung up on bringing too many other blacks along."

One male banker with an MBA at the vice-president level in a money center bank actually was advised by his supervisors that he was spending too much time with other blacks in the bank and that unless he curtailed his activities, his future at the bank would be jeopardized. In other words, at a minimum he could not expect any further promotions. This young man, who was in his middle thirties, commenting on his probable promotion freeze, related this story:

> All I was doing was attempting to organize blacks in the bank for the purpose of networking, sharing information [which whites do all the time and take for granted] and professional development for strategies for success enhancement.
>
> While whites get together in small groups constantly, at lunch, dinner, cocktails, at a party, when they see blacks doing this in groups larger than two people, they seem to fear that there is a rebellion cooking.
>
> Obviously, blacks talk about their problems when they get together, just as whites do; but mostly we are exchanging ideas and experiences in an effort to develop strategies for success in the bank. *What* we are doing, and what they *think* we are doing, are two different things.
>
> Nonetheless, they were adamant about their position regarding this issue, and I felt they wanted my soul, rather than my performance. My performance had always been outstanding. I did not feel I should have to give them my soul, so I resigned from the bank. Fortunately, I have another job that I think has greater potential than that which I could foresee at that bank, both in earnings and responsibilities.

It is clear from the above scenarios that at best, blacks in the banking industry function in a hostile environment. Working in an inhospitable environment is obviously not unique to blacks in the banking or any other industry. It should be remembered that the 73 successful executives described by Lombardo and McCall each had endured hostile environments in their efforts to climb the success ladder. In this regard, it should be further remembered that the most frequent intolerable boss that they had encountered was the "Snake-in-the-Grass."

From the description of the behavior of the bosses to which our interviewees have been subjected, Dr. Michael Maccoby in his book, *Gamesman* (1976), would label them "foxes." In his effort to describe the modern corporate gamesmen, he defined the foxes as "managers who were cunning and secretive, with strong exploitative, narcissistic, and sadistic-authoritarian tendencies."[2]

Superimpose racism on top of the above forces and one gets a clearer picture of the problems blacks must endure to succeed in the banking industry.

NOTES

1. Gorda W. Bowman, "What Helps or Harms Promotability, Paths Toward Personal Progress," *Harvard Business Review* (1982): 94.
2. Michael Maccoby, *The Gamesman* (New York: Simon and Schuster, 1970), p. 80.

5

IS THERE A MENTOR
OUT THERE FOR ME?

From a semantic point of view, the concept of a mentor is relatively new. Only within the last decade has it been written about for public consumption. Nevertheless if we look beyond the semantics, mentors, by other names, have been around for as long as people have worked in organizations. These individuals have been called "guardian angels," "protectors," "sponsors," "preceptors," and even "godfathers." These names, however, were almost never used in official circles. By whatever name, they were the power link in the "old boy network." Obviously, the old boy network was not exclusively mentors, but generally it was the mentor who could cause things to happen when the need arose.

In recent years there has been a plethora of articles regarding the concept of mentors. While in the past the concept was referred to in almost "hush-hush" tones, today, like sex, it is no longer talked about only "behind the scenes." It is written about as a legitimate relationship in the corporate world in the most respected periodicals, among which are the *Harvard Business Review* and *Supervisory Management* and similar high quality publications.

In this chapter, we will explore whether or not mentors are necessary in one's career development in the corporation; how to acquire one; whether or not one is deemed desirable; where mentors are most likely to be found; and how to get the most out of them if one happens to have one or more.

As a part of this discussion, we will focus on the experience of blacks with and without mentors in the banking industry, their perception of the value of mentors, and finally how those who have them got them.

IS A MENTOR REALLY NECESSARY?

Mentors are persons who have risen to relative power positions within the corporation and who can be of valuable assistance to a person of lower rank who is trying to climb the corporate ladder. Many people go through their corporate life without ever having a mentor. Many, at least in the past, did not know what the concept of mentor meant, or understand why some of their associates continued to move above them up the ladder, sometimes apparently without regard to their level of work efficiency or productivity.

Those persons falling into the latter class no doubt had mentors who assisted them quietly and inconspicuously, but effectively. For example, when asked if he had a mentor, a 28-year-old black MBA loan officer in a Southeastern bank said:

> No, I do not have a mentor. However, the whites have mentors when they walk in the door. That's often the way they got their job. They knew somebody who was already in the bank and that person helped them move up. If they don't know the person directly, they know that person's father, grandfather or somebody important, so that helps move them up the ladder quickly, whereas with us [blacks], it's a "proving thing" everyday. It really hurts if you don't have a person who's looking out for you and trying to help you move up the ladder.

While this banker's perception that all whites have mentors when they come into the bank may be somewhat at variance with reality, it is not too far off target. In this regard, Gerald R. Roache, in a 1977 survey of successful corporate executives who had mentors, found that they earned more money at a younger age, were more likely to follow a systematic career plan, and, in general, were more happy with their work than those who did not have mentors.[1]

Significantly, however, while those with mentors tended to rise faster in the corporate hierarchy, they personally felt that they could have succeeded without one. They felt that the most important success criteria were such personal characteristics as the ability to make decisions, motivation, the ability to motivate others, the ability to lead, the ability to complete assignments, a high energy level, and a willingness to work long hours.[2]

Roache also found that, in general, women tended to have more mentors than men, three-to-two respectively.[3]

While women may have more mentors than men, we emphasize that females are likely to encounter a more complex relationship with them when the mentors are male. As pointed out in greater detail later in this chapter, females with male mentors place themselves at certain risk. Accordingly, the relationship should be managed with great care. Another Southeastern banker, when asked if he had observed whether or not blacks have mentors, said:

> At my bank, which is probably much more conservative than most banks, there aren't many blacks. Of the blacks that are there, most do not have mentors. There are a couple that do have mentors and they are moving up the ladder quite well.

While the mentor may no longer be a strictly private phenomenon, he or she is not one who publicly holds himself or herself out as a person available to help someone. In this respect, the mentor-mentee relationship may be known through the grapevine, but in most firms the relationship is rarely openly displayed. In general, the mentor acts behind the scenes in ways that are not always obvious.

A mentor can do many things for a mentee. Most of a mentor's activities can be classified under the category of career assistance. A mentor can assist a mentee with the all important task of planning his or her career, providing timely information regarding opportunities, assisting with technical aspects of the mentee's job, and helping the mentee approach problems which he or she encounters in his or her job activities.

We emphasize that the mentor should not be expected to help a sloppy, undeserving employee with his or her self-induced problems, although there are those who do so. The kinds of problems the mentor can be expected to assist a mentee with are ones over which the mentee has no control. There are likely to be many of those.

In general, when the prospective mentee has demonstrated that he or she is a quality employee, the mentor can provide that extra "push" to get the mentee over the next hurdle and up the career ladder.

Perhaps one of the most systematic approaches to the management of the mentor-mentee relationship is that utilized by the Jewel Companies of Chicago. In a 1978 article appearing in the *Harvard Business Review*, Collins and Scott described the details of a formal program, planned and managed by the Jewel Companies. The Companies assigned mentors to every new MBA entering the company, beginning in 1931. All successive presidents and senior officers have evolved from this strategy.[4]

THE MENTOR-MENTEE RELATIONSHIP

The mentor-mentee relationship is generally a personal one. It may have stemmed from a relationship that existed between the mentor and someone who is close to the mentee, such as a relative, friend, or business associates. This obviously is the easiest relationship to establish and maintain. It may have been long-standing, perhaps even for generations, or it may be new. This has been the most prevalent type relationship between the mentor and the mentee. It was personal and, thus, was generally kept beyond the purview of the official business association.

These relationships were established at social clubs, church or school affiliations, recreational clubs (that is, golf, tennis, racquetball), etc. They are by nature stronger than official business interrelations. This stems from the fact that they grow out of an environment of mutual fun and relaxation, free of the tension and, often, the intrigue of office politics.

If the mentor relationship is not established before one becomes an employee of an institution, the question becomes, how does one go about obtaining a mentor? Does one go up to a person and say, "Will you be my mentor?" That approach may work; however, such an approach is tantamount to asking a lady (or a man) of casual acquaintance, "Will you be my lover tonight?" The answer *may* be yes; but it is more likely to be a look of astonishment, a stammering, meaningless, evasive answer, or a forthright "No."

The relationship between a mentor and a mentee must be based upon a foundation of trust, established over some time period, either by virtue of a prior relationship or as a result of a sustained and proven relationship orchestrated by the mentee. Even when the mentor-mentee relationship exists, the word "mentor" or "mentee" may never be directly spoken in the interaction between the persons involved. The relationship may be a solid one, but because it is informal and unofficial it is not advertised.

THE RELATIONSHIP – ON WHOSE INITIATIVE?

We emphasize here that the responsibility for initiating the relationship is upon the shoulders of the prospective mentee, not with the mentor. Obviously, there are situations in which the mentor may be the initiator, in which case the mentee can consider himself or herself fortunate. But to "lay back" and expect the mentor to create the relationship is to risk not getting one.

Obviously, the mentor will determine whether or not the relationship will exist, but he or she will be motivated to adopt the mentee only after the latter has demonstrated that he or she is the kind of person with which the mentor would enjoy working.

Most blacks enter industry without "prearranged mentors." Given contemporary American mores which still largely cause blacks and whites to go their separate ways after five o'clock, the question becomes how is a black expected to secure a mentor unless that mentor happens to be black?

IS THERE A MENTOR FOR EVERYONE?

While it is more difficult to secure a mentor when it is not pre-arranged, or when the normal social patterns do not lend themselves to natural settings within which a mentor relationship can be cultivated, blacks in industry should be aware that they are not alone in not having mentors when they enter the industrial job market. The precise percentage of employees in banking or any industry who have mentors is unknown, but it is reasonable to assume that those with mentors are still a relatively small minority, both white and black. If we accept this assumption, even many white employees are likely never to enjoy the privilege of having a mentor.

This assumption follows logically from the pyramid shape of the organization chart. The nature of the industrial organization is that there can be only a few persons at the top. Since succession management cannot outnumber the required number of top level officers in the organization, there can be only a few of those at the lower levels of the organization who can effectively be groomed to succeed upper level management. Under this premise, the mentor is likely to be very selective as to those persons whom he or she adopts as mentees. In other words, the competition for the attention of the mentor is likely to be quite keen, depending upon how much "clout" he or she is perceived to have.

THE ELUSIVE MENTOR – SOME APPROACHES

Given the above assumptions, the only recourse that most blacks and many whites have in their pursuit of a mentor is to develop and deftly utilize superior job and social skills.

With respect to job skills, for example, one banker suggested this approach to finding a mentor:

> Each time a person seeking a mentor prepares a written report, he can, in the normal course of business practice, send a copy to persons outside of his immediate department who might have an interest in the subject without violating organizational lines. If a "power broker" happens to logically be on the list, no one can raise eyebrows for your having sent him a copy. *The secret is not to be obvious in the pursuit of a mentor.*

A female vice-president of a Midwestern bank offered this advice:

> You have to be creative and take initiatives and you have to take some risks. For example, find out who the "power brokers" are in your organization, and find out what their official responsibilities are. Create a situation, over coffee, or another natural situation within which you can tell him how interested you are in his area of responsibility. It must be both genuine and a natural learning opportunity for you. If it's artificial, your motives will be spotted immediately and you'll be thrown out on your ear. Offer to do a special research project for him on an issue of interest to him. Do it on your own time if necessary. Since the project is in his interest, and since he perceives that your motives are to learn as much as you can about his area, he is rarely likely to turn you down. But then do a *jam-up* job for him! This opens the door and it's up to you to keep building

upon that relationship. When he is convinced that you're a good risk, you may have yourself a mentor; but don't expect to walk in his office one day and hear him announcing, "I've decided to be your mentor." If he becomes your mentor, he won't have to announce it; you will know it. If not, you more than likely do not deserve a mentor. There is no room for intellectual density in this environment, but don't expect to be adopted immediately. Relationship development takes time and it cannot be rushed. You can bet he is going to look you over and over again before he decides to take risks with you.

In addition, you can never take the relationship for granted. For example, don't expect him to stick his neck out for you when you're wrong. And don't create a situation and then go to him asking him to bail you out. Go to him before a situation erupts and talk the matter over with him and get his advice before you act. Finally, don't go to him with frivolous matters. His time is valuable and if you waste it, he's likely to cut you off.

When asked how he was able to get mentors, one black employment manager at a money center bank who said he has had mentors since he first entered banking, had this to say:

I think it is based upon a lot of things, your schooling, the people you were *brought up with*, the environment within which you developed your life goals, how you view yourself, how you interact with others, etc. As for my particular success, I think it stems from my days in high school and college, where I had to learn that if I was going to succeed (being the only black in most of my classes), I needed some interaction with my peers. That meant that I had to learn how to deal with them and, in fact, that's just what I mean, *learn to deal with them*. I'm going to have to figure out how to get them to like me and to give me their information too. Once you master the technique of dealing with them, then getting mentors is just an extension of that technique.

While one may have more chances to cultivate a mentor in the normal course of one's official job, perhaps the most effective approach is the skillful and timely use of one's social skills. *It is axiomatic that more deals are cut on the golf course or over drinks than are cut in the office.* This is why business enterprises routinely pay club and association dues for their officers and salesmen. This gives them an opportunity to get to know possible clients on a social basis. This gives them a leg up when they are ready to compete head to head for business the next day at the office.

While the social route is perhaps the most effective approach in the pursuit of a mentor, black Americans are placed at a distinct disadvantage in this arena because of the prevailing social mores of U.S. society. With notable exceptions, white America continues to eschew genuine, relaxed social interaction with blacks and other minority Americans. This was borne out by our respondents' revelation that almost seven out of ten black bankers say they are not invited by either their supervisors or their peers *to other than official functions.*

THE FRUSTRATIONS – ARE THEY WORTH IT?

Nevertheless, like other difficult challenges which black Americans face, *the social inclusion challenge*, while clearly more difficult, is one that can and should be *creatively* approached and constantly worked at, notwithstanding its inherent frustrations. Trying to win acceptance of those who hold the reins of power against their will is difficult beyond imagination. One's self-esteem is severely challenged under these conditions.

Accordingly, it was not surprising to find that a number of black bankers rejected the mentor concept, as exemplified by a female West Coast banker, who took the position that:

> I make sure I do my work so they can't find any fault with that, and at the end of the day, I let them go their way and I go mine. In fact, by the end of the day, I am tired of being with them, because of their attitudes. I want to go somewhere that I can let my hair down and relax. With them, you've got to be constantly on guard, because they're constantly observing you for positions or language that may suggest that you aren't like them, and that's what they require of you for acceptance. You must be like them.

This is both a predictable and an understandable attitude, given the trauma to one's ego in the above scenario. However, as plausible as this attitude may appear, it ignores fundamental organization behavior. There is a considerable body of research which concludes that all organizations, large and small, formal and informal, tend to have personality and behavior norms, whether the group is Sunday school teachers, streetwalkers, or I.B.M. Any members of the group who, for whatever reason, do not deport themselves in accordance with the organizational norms, will either be ostracized by the group or leave because of frustration. If one doubts this premise, he or she should simply reflect for a moment on his or her childhood or current friendship circle. There is a similarity of behavior patterns. This is a human tendency that supercedes race or ethnicity.

The complexity of the behavior norms in industry in general, and banking in particular, is compounded by racism. Nonetheless, there are outstanding examples (although perhaps not in large numbers) of blacks in all aspects of U.S. life who have achieved in spite of intense racism. The challenge to blacks in the banking industry is to achieve, as others have, in spite of racist conditions.

In this regard, we found examples of blacks (both men and women) who are making it in the banking industry in spite of racism. These bankers tended to take the attitude that if a black is to succeed in the banking industry at this stage in history, he or she has to, in the words of one male vice-president in a regional bank:

> Build a steel stage around his ego, let both implicit and explicit racist darts bounce off rather than puncture his skin. He has to have the eyes of an owl by night and an eagle by day. He has to have the ears of a jack rabbit, and the "gut feel" of a politician to gauge what's happening around him. He has to be "super good" at his job and work like hell. That's just for starters. He then has to figure out how to get into the sociopolitical system. And that's the most difficult thing for him to do. Nothing is guaranteed, but what you've got to do is act like you belong wherever you happen to be. Don't be timid or stand back and expect to be invited into the conversation. Move in. It may be awkward at first, but keep it up. Both they and you will get used to your being a part of the conversation. Or, don't wait until everybody has gone to lunch without you and pout because you weren't invited. Figure out who the informal leader in the group is and go to him early and invite him to lunch, or say "I'd like to join you guys at lunch." I have yet to be turned down on deals like that, not because they genuinely wanted to invite me, but they were in a position that made it awkward to say no. But if I were turned down, I'll keep it up until they begin to include me.
>
> Also, I make it a point to attend every optional social function that I can, especially if I expect certain power brokers to be there.

I don't always have fun, but I go anyway. That's the only way for you to get to know them and for them to get to know you. And once they get to know you where they feel that they can laugh with you and you with them, then you have reached a sort of *comfort level* that more than likely will get you invited routinely. You'd be surprised at what you might pick up after they get a few drinks under their belts. Just one piece of information may be worth the trouble of going to that party.

MENTORS – WHERE DO YOU FIND THEM?

Mentors come in a variety of settings and configurations. They may be male or female, black or white, within or without your department, inside your organization or in a totally different one. They may be in your industry or another industry. A mentor may be a peer or a higher level officer. He may be a person with official power, or someone who may only have relevant information or wisdom, each of which may be a source of power. The mentor may possess several attributes of value to a mentee, or he may be one-dimensional. A person may have one or several mentors.[5]

With respect to race, our field interviews predictably revealed that currently for blacks who have them, most mentors are white. This naturally follows from the fact that there are still so few blacks *in a position* to become effective mentors. There seemed to be a strong desire for black mentors, however, on the part of many of our interviewees, although this attitude was not universal.

In this regard, when asked if he had a mentor, one black male vice-president and loan officer of a West Coast bank said:

Yes, I have a mentor who, thank God, is black. It is very critical in this particular industry for us to have mentors who are black, if at all possible, because, more than likely, the black mentor would have gone down the same road that we are approaching. . . . I have been in several situations that I felt were racially related. When these things happen to me, I get on the phone and say, "Hey look, this is the situation, . . . He'd say, let me tell you my experience, I've been down that road, and this is how you deal with it. . . ."

Whether one's mentor is black or white, higher level or peer level, the most important criterion for determining the value of that mentor is to assess the degree of mutual trust existing between the mentor and oneself. In the first instance, the mentor is not likely to get involved in a substantive manner unless he feels that he can trust the mentee. Obviously, such trust should flow both ways.

THE MENTOR – GETTING THE MOST OUT OF HIM/HER

A mentor should not be expected to plunge in with both feet and begin throwing his or her weight around on behalf of a mentee as soon as they meet. The mentor-mentee relationship, of necessity, is generally a slowly emerging one. The mentor wants to make certain that he or she understands the nature of the risks and demands that may be made as a result of the relationship.

To keep the relationship viable, the mentee should communicate with the mentor as frequently as necessary without becoming a pest so as to keep the communication system fluid. The mentor's advice and influence should be sought regarding only issues which the mentee can handle in no other way.

While the mentee is rarely in a position to reciprocate for the advice and influence directed his or her way by the mentor, the creative and resourceful mentee will be on the lookout for ways to be of assistance to the mentor. While the mentor is not likely to expect reciprocal favors for his mentorship, it is just good human relations in marketing oneself to show one's appreciation, when opportunities present themselves.

ABUSING THE RELATIONSHIP

Perhaps the most important criterion for sustained mutual relations between one's mentor and oneself is *trust*. There is obvious risk associated with a mentor's efforts to assist a mentee. If a mentor does something on behalf of a mentee, only to hear it throughout the bank, the chances are that that mentee will be left "out in the cold" the next time he or she needs assistance. Violating the mentor's trust is the ultimate abuse of the mentor-mentee relationship. This was illustrated by a black male banker in an East Coast bank who is in a position to serve as a mentor. When asked if he was a mentor to younger bankers in his bank, he said:

I have served as a mentor and I am going to continue to try in the future, but in an effort to help a young banker recently, I passed on some valuable information that was important to him in his efforts to win a promotion, only to be confronted by some of my white peers that I had passed on the information. So I got my ass burned for trying to help a brother, who violated my trust. So I've pulled back from my role as a mentor for a while. I know I should do it and I am going to get back out there. But I'm going to be much more selective as to who I'm going to help than I formerly was.

A number of our interviewees indicated that they had black mentors and were proud to have them. However, there were other interviewees who indicated that when some blacks reach high levels of responsibility they become inaccessible. "They take the attitude that I got mine, you get yours." We heard this attitude expressed a number of times.

SECURING AND MANAGING THE RELATIONSHIP – SOME SUGGESTIONS

On balance, our research suggests that a mentor can be useful in developing one's career. However, it is still very difficult for the average black American to obtain one. As difficult as it is, however, we believe the potential benefits are worth the effort. Accordingly, we are setting forth below a list of approaches which may be useful to those who may wish to seek out a mentor within their organization.

1. The first order of business is to conduct a systematic appraisal of the environment. Find out who the movers and shakers are among peers and among upper level management.
2. Decide which one or combination of the movers and shakers would be most helpful in your career pursuit.
3. Typically, the prospective mentee must take the initiative in establishing a mentor-mentee relationship. The best approach is to genuinely seek advice about a particular problem or issue related to your work.
4. Don't expect one mentor to serve all your needs. You may need two or more.

5. Be subtle, genuine, and low key in your approach to the prospective mentor. This is not a task for the obtuse.
6. Don't expect to be successful each time you seek out a mentor. Even Babe Ruth struck out more often than he hit home runs.
7. Actively participate in social functions, both formal and informal. This is where you are likely to make the most headway.
8. Don't expect every mentor-mentee relationship to be permanent. Most such relationships are transitory. In fact, they're like true friends, few and far between.
9. Unless the mentor-mentee relationship is orchestrated by the institution, keep the relationship in confidence.
10. Remember, the most productive mentor-mentee relationship must be built upon mutual trust.
11. Perhaps the most difficult relationship to establish and sustain is the one in which the prospective mentee is female and the prospective mentor is male. Considerable sophistication on the part of both the mentor and the mentee is required to successfully develop and sustain this relationship because vicious rumors are an ever present risk. Mary Cunningham, formerly of the Bendix Corporation, is a prime example of this phenomenon. Fortunately, hers had a happy ending. But most female mentees cannot marry the boss.[6]
12. Finally, one should deport oneself with a high self-image and self-confidence. Behave as though you belong where you are, you have something to offer, and the relationship will not be only one way. Nobody likes to take on a "drag."

NOTES

1. Gerald Roach, "Much Ado About Mentors," *Harvard Business Review* 57 (January-February 1979): 16.

2. Ibid., p. 20.

3. Ibid., p. 24.

4. G. C. Collins and Patricia Scott, "Everyone Who Makes It Has a Mentor," *Harvard Business Review* 56 (July-August 1978): 135.

5. Daniel Lea and Zandy B. Leibowitz, "Mentor: Would You Know One If You Saw One?" *Supervisory Management* 15 (April 1983): 34.

6. Mary Cunningham was a young attractive MBA from a prestigious business school who was elevated from Special Assistant to the President of the Bendix Corporation, to Executive Vice-President in charge of corporate planning.

After three years out of the Harvard Business School and a like number of years of tenure with the Bendix Corporation, this elevation caused vicious rumors that reached all the way to the board of directors. These rumors caused her resignation and badly scarred the reputation of the president, Mr. Agee. See: "Executive Sweet at Bendix," *Newsweek*, Vol. 96, Dec. 15, 1980, p. 84 (1); "Godfathers and Gossips" (female executives) *Industry Week*, Vol. 207, Oct. 27, 1980, p. 172 (1); Bendix Abuse, "Resignation of Mary Cunningham," *Time*, Vol. 116, Oct. 6, 1980, p. 83 (1); "Upheaval at Bendix," *Fortune*, Nov. 3, 1980, p. 48; and "Things the B-School Never Taught," *Fortune*, November 3, 1980, p. 53.

6

INSIDE AND OUTSIDE
THE NETWORKS—
WHO'S IN
AND WHO'S OUT?

Like mentoring, networking has only recently come out of the underground. However, it is not new as a phenomenon. It has always been and perhaps will always be a part of organizational dynamics. Only recently, however, has it been openly discussed and widely written about under the fashionable name networking.[1]

While mentors and mentees function in a vertical relationship, networking, with notable exceptions, functions in a horizontal relationship. The mentor is typically one with official power. The network cohort or contact is generally perceived as one possessing primarily relevant experience and/or information. In this regard, it should be emphasized that relevant experience and information may be the most powerful tools in the corporate environment. Thus, the art of networking may be one of the most important skills at the disposal of a person seeking to work his way up the corporate ladder.

When this research project was being conceptualized we were not aware that networking would become such an important issue in the research. It was only after we began to analyze the data from both the questionnaire and the interviews that it became evident that networking was one of the most important issues affecting the success/failure of those seeking to find their way up the corporate ladder.

In this chapter, we will explore the rationale for networking, the art of selecting network cohorts, the several organizational structures of networking as well as the experience of our respondents with networking.

NETWORKING – WHY BOTHER?

Networking by whatever name is the art of using one's social and political skills to advance oneself in the corporate environment. Like it or not, politics is an all pervasive phenomenon in the corporate structure.

In this regard, Chester Berger, author of *Survival in the Executive Jungle*, warns that:

> Office politics exist in every company, and at every level. They're the inevitable concomitant of a competitive economy. I've known more than one hundred corporations from the inside, but never one where office politics were absent. So don't expect to escape it in your own company. The innocent young man who wishes he could simply concentrate on his job, and ignore his personal relationships, is day dreaming.[2]

A networking *cohort*, commonly called a *contact*, is often myopically referred to as "someone you can call upon to do something for you." Realistically, however, it should be emphasized that a network is a two-way communication system.

Typically, each member must be perceived as being able to do something for each other. An unidirectional network cannot be sustained over time. As for the importance of networking, the reader need only refer back to Chapter 1, in which our respondents indicated that their most important problem is "not knowing what's going on in the organization," and to Chapter 4, in which they indicated that the most important promotion criterion is "who you know," or "office politics."

"Not knowing what's going on" and "not knowing anybody" are both on the negative side of the networking coin. On the positive side is "knowing what's going on" and "knowing somebody."

Mention connections or the "old boy network" to the average red-blooded American businessman and you may get a grimace. The words *can* connote low deals, back scratching, bumbling relatives eased onto the payroll. You're also likely to get a defensive response from the average executive, such as, "We don't play the game that way." And yet, the still small voice of reality whispers, contacts *are* important. Prod the average executive a bit and he will admit as much.[3]

If our respondents are on target with respect to networking, the most important benefit of this phenomenon is the *flow of information*. It is this information flow that is the power base of networking.

If relevant information is perceived as so very important in an organizational context, persons possessing it are likely to guard it zealously. Only those considered their most trusted confidants are likely to become privy to this prized possession.

Information may fall into a number of categories. Among these is information regarding job opportunities that are on the horizon, that is, before they become public; information regarding the idiosyncrasies of the boss, that is, what really turns him on or off, what his management style is, and what his personal and business objectives are; what the boss's source of power is; who he leans on or respects most in the department; whether or not the boss is on a fast track or has topped out. Obviously, given enough time, one can learn much of the above through careful observation. The quickest and most effective way to learn the above, however, is from peers who are privy to that information.

One can also learn what is going on outside the immediate department through networking: who the movers and shakers are and what the social and political alliances are, and what is happening to the company in general.

In addition to information regarding organizational dynamics, networking can become a source of information about technical aspects of one's particular job. There are occasional situations when one needs help with the technology of a particular job and may feel insecure asking the boss. A trusted peer usually is the best alternative in situations such as these. Through networking one can get insights into career options that may not flow directly from one's boss, although they should.

Because problems are inherent in all organizational structures, networking can enable one to uncover alternative approaches to those problems. In general, most organizations foster a pattern of problems that tend to repeat themselves. Most such problems are people problems. Since people problems are not likely to be unique, or even new in any given organizational structure, it stands to reason that someone has experienced those problems before and is likely to have some idea as to how a given problem might be effectively approached.

Finally, even when one's network cohort cannot contribute to the solution of a problem, frequently, the emotional release associated with talking to someone who understands and empathizes can relieve considerable tension.

One young male banker, who had been out of the bank training program for about two years, recalled his networking experience beginning during the training program:

> You had to talk to other trainees because you weren't getting any help from the top. So networking was vital. A young black person coming into the industry ought to immediately try to plug into one of the black networks inside and outside of the bank. . . .

Another high ranking male banker with more than 100 persons working for him said:

> My participation in the local chapter and the national level of the National Association of Urban Bankers has been vitally important to me in my career development. I'm active now and have been active since its inception and will continue to be active.

NETWORKING – IS BIG BROTHER WATCHING?

One of the most bewildering phenomena that we encountered in our field research was the widespread perception of a negative attitude of management toward blacks who seek to network in the same manner as their white peers. We found this phenomenon in all sections of the country, although it was not universal.

SOME POSITIVE SUPPORT OF NETWORKING

On the other hand, we also found that a number of banks were *passively supportive* of black bankers' efforts to network, but actively supported those who participated in the NAUB, both locally and nationally.

An example of this positive support of NAUB is the support that was given the current (1983-84) national president by his employer. His bank not only gave him ample free time to devote to the business of the organization but also provided him with a generous travel fund that permitted him to travel throughout the country visiting and meeting with chapters on their home grounds. He indicated that his bank felt that the objectives of the NAUB were little different from those of the National Organization of Bank Women, and similar organizations. They each are seeking to share experiences and information that may enhance their careers. A casual perusal of the local and national NAUB programs illustrates the career development orientation of this organization. While we were visiting the West Coast, one of the major banks was serving as host at a major reception for NAUB in the Los Angeles area. In addition, many of the banks pay the travel and related costs to conventions of NAUB members who are employees of the respective banks just as they do for all other banking subsets.

Perhaps the most innovative network structure we uncovered in our research was that conceived and executed by Security Pacific National Bank of Los Angeles.

Faced with excessive minority officer turnover this bank, instead of permitting the condition to persist, organized a formal program of minority-manager career seminars and formal networks that successfully reduced the turnover problem.

The Career Strategies Program for Black Managers was handled by an outside consultant. These seminars covered the classical issues that typically are associated with successful career development.

Next, the bank created and launched a program called BOSS, Black Officers Support System. BOSS had two purposes. First, it was to assist in the recruitment and retention of black officers. Second, the members of BOSS were to encourage black officers to set and meet high standards of performance and to pursue career opportunities within the bank and under its corporate umbrella.

The network structure of BOSS was bank wide. BOSS engaged in four principal functions. It: (1) initiated a buddy system for new black management trainees; (2) encouraged and assisted its members in getting involved in the community, a policy which the bank encouraged; (3) assisted members with technical problems associated with their job; and (4) perhaps as its most important function, members generally shared experiences with each other.

Based upon the success of BOSS, similar networks are being established for Hispanic and Asian Americans.

According to Ms. Hayes, Vice-President for Employee Relations at Security Pacific, "We see the program described above as part of a total approach to affirmative action — one that goes beyond just hiring."[4]

SOME BANKS SEEK TO THWART NETWORKING

While Security Pacific has launched an innovative and positive program to facilitate career development of minorities, our research suggests that there is an indeterminant number of banks that seek to thwart efforts of their black managers to network.

This issue of management's negative reaction to black networking was not a part of the original research design. Instead, it was uncovered in our semi-structured open-ended questionnaire which we utilized in the personal interviews. Therefore, we did not seek to definitively measure how widespread the negative reaction to networking by black bankers is in the industry. We are confident however, that while it may not be the prevailing attitude in the industry, it is prevalent enough to be easily discerned in all sections of the country, although its intensity varies from place to place.

As evidence of this negative phenomenon, one male vice-president of a regional bank said:

Anytime more than two of us get together while on the job, they get concerned. It doesn't matter what we are talking about. We can be talking about baseball, the party we had last night, or how to improve a particular system or approach a problem in the course of our duties; they just seem to get nervous under those conditions. You can see them staring at you in much the same manner that they did in the South during the segregation era when a black showed up in an area where they thought he did not belong. The irony of this phenomenon is that whites openly and obviously network all the time. You see it all around you. In fact, it is taken for granted. They are expected to network and they do. Unfortunately, they attribute ulterior motives to blacks when they attempt to network. So you see, this is the most blatant type of racism.

Another female, assistant vice-president of a regional money center bank told of how her bank had effectively thwarted its black employees' attempt at networking.

> Many of us had gotten together to more or less inform each other, work to help one another and management became aware of it and squashed it. They started transferring people, scaring them with threats of termination, indirectly, just to the degree that they could get away with it. . . . That broke up our effort.

Another vice-president male banker of a money center bank elected to resign rather than adhere to the bank's admonishment that he should refrain from his efforts to promote networking among blacks in the bank.

As the above experiences indicate, the practice seems widespread that the industry reacts to black attempts to emulate the networking behavior of their white peers with a severe case of racism and cynicism bordering on paranoia. This approach to black networking on the part of the industry is clearly counterproductive for the development of a loyal and productive cadre of black bankers. It seems to us that this problem deserves careful consideration and a positive course of action from top management.

NETWORKING – HOW DO I GET IN?

Developing a network and developing a mentor-mentee relationship require similar interpersonal, social, and political skills. Each relationship requires the initiative of the person desiring the relationship. One cannot "lay back," expecting the relationship to be handed to him. The mentor-mentee relationship is generally vertical in structure, the network relationship generally horizontal, or among persons on the same career level. Each of them is developed and sustained on the principle that each participant brings something to the table. This latter characteristic, however, is likely to be more prevalent in the network relationship than in the mentor-mentee relationship. The mentor may be satisfied with the pride of having helped a young person succeed, or he may seek to strengthen future management of the organization, for which he may have a major interest. He may not ever expect to receive any direct benefits from the mentee.

The network relationship, however, requires a perception on the part of each participant that each is getting as much as one is giving if the relationship is to be sustained over time. Accordingly, if one is to get the most out of a relationship, one must be constantly on the alert for ways to be of assistance to those in the network. The person who never has anything to offer the relationship is likely to be perceived as a "drag," and sooner or later will be ostracized by the group.

The strategy for getting into a network depends upon the nature of the network one seeks to enter. In other words, is the network among peers in the department or in another department, inside the organization or in another organization? Is the network cohort an individual or an organization?

Our research reveals that the most difficult network for black Americans to break into is that of their white peers. This was the conclusion which resulted from both the mail questionnaire and the personal interviews.

In our efforts to interpret the "peer relationship" component of our mail questionnaire, we discovered that the questions were ambiguous with respect to race. In other words, we had no way of determining whether the respondents' peers were black or white or both. Given our findings that blacks have considerable difficulty in establishing genuine mutual relationships with their white peers in the industry, it makes a difference in our interpretation of the responses whether our respondents were referring to their white or black peers or a combination of both. It became clear from our mail questionnaire that our respondents gave their overall peer relationship a 5.45 rating, which suggests that this relationship is essentially bland, that is, not good, but not bad.

The lowest rating on the satisfaction scale was for the statement, "My peers often invite me to social functions outside the bank." In this regard, the fact that six out of ten respondents say they were not invited to outside social functions by their peers suggests that our respondents were probably largely referring to their white peers. Since the social outlet is perhaps the most fluid communication system, this means that most of our respondents are excluded from this system. If we accept the assumption that one needs to be plugged into the communication system to know what is going on, this would tend to confirm the conclusion of our respondents that they do not know what's going on in the organization.

As for the technique for getting into this less than hospitable environment, as previously stated, it obviously is not easy. However, those respondents who were successful in breaking into this system basically did not allow their egos to get in the way, displayed a high self-image, deported themselves as though they belonged wherever they happened to be, creatively but unobtrusively asserted themselves into one-on-one and group conversations, deftly took the initiative in inviting themselves into whatever was going on around them, that is, going to lunch, or to coffee, taking in the after work drink or just a "bull" session. This may be awkward at first, but if persistent, ultimately a "comfort level" will be reached that will make the process almost as natural as going to the copy machine.

NETWORKING WITH WHOM? OR WHO'S IN?

Networking can be exercised on several levels. Beginning within one's own department, one can network with both minority and white peers. The process can and should include both office situations and after work functions. Outside the department one can network with peers whose job interests are the same. While one may cultivate a variety of peer contacts, one should take care to be aware of those who appear to be on the fast track. Those persons on the fast track generally are identifiable through the "grapevine." These people tend to behave as though they're going to "inherit the earth" and the chances are, they will. Nonverbal signals are generally quite obvious with respect to who is (and who is not) on the fast track. We found many instances among our interviewees in which they were quite aware of the "fair haired boys" and the "golden haired girls" in their organization. This was the rule rather than the exception.

Networking with someone on a higher level than one's self is possible, but is more complex. This is normally a mentor-mentee relationship. However, one should not concentrate on the type of relationship that might develop, but rather on developing that relationship whether it be peer or mentor-mentee in structure.

What might be overlooked, however, particularly for black Americans, is an opportunity to network with someone below one's organizational level. Information which is one of the principal objectives of networking has a way of filtering through secretaries, for example, before it gets to other official levels. While white Americans may not find it necessary to network across vertical organizational levels, at this point in history, black Americans may find that it is a luxury they can ill afford.

Finally, a rich source of networking, particularly for black Americans, is professional and social organizations outside the bank. We found numerous instances of both male and female bankers who said that they could not have made it without the networking with outside professional and social organizations.

One female banker in a money center bank put it this way:

I network with several different organizations. The NAUB, the black accountants, the concerned black executives and the Black MBAs. Any time I come across a problem on which I need help, I just pick up the phone and call the appropriate contact. My boss is often surprised when he gives me an assignment, expecting me to fail, only to be presented with a correct and viable solution, on time. There isn't anything in this bank that I can't find someone in my network that knows about it. So you see, I network constantly.

NETWORKING – WHO'S OUT?

Selecting a mutually beneficial network cohort is little different from selecting one's friends. For best results, one should seek alliances with persons who are similarly motivated and are striving to reach the same kind of goals. Conversely, one should avoid persons who seek to progress on politics alone, or who never bring anything to the table.

It is a truism that corporate life functions within a political milieu. Accordingly, very little can be accomplished without an understanding of the political alliances that are operational within the organization. One should be aware, however, that there are risk-reward systems associated with the political alliances. One has the option of aligning oneself with a given political faction within his organization. If the leader of that faction falls out of favor with the power structure, however, those associated with that faction are likely to suffer the same fate as the leader, that is, that person may be shunted aside without a substantive job, or may even be fired.

One regional center male banker cited this example:

> It just so happened the man who brought me into the bank was tapped to be president. I have maintained a good relationship with him. So I now have the kind of leverage in my job that comes with the perception throughout the bank that I have a line straight to the president. I can get a lot of things done that I couldn't otherwise accomplish without this perception throughout the bank.
>
> That's the positive side of being plugged into the political network. On the other hand, I have seen situations in which the leader of a faction lost a power struggle and was fired. All of his cronies were fired or resigned as well. So you see, one has to be very careful in aligning himself with particular political factions, especially if that alignment is known throughout the bank. I'm not saying don't ever do it. What I am saying is, however, you had better know what you're doing when you go public with your political alliances.

NOTES

1.   Walter Kiechell III, "The Care and Feeding of Contacts," *Fortune* 105 (February 8, 1982): 119.

2.   Chester Berger, *Survival in the Executive Jungle* (New York: MacMillan, 1964), p. 1.

3.   Kiechell, "The Care and Feeding of Contacts," p. 120.

4.   Kathleen C. Hayes, "If Minorities Quit, Spirit of Affirmative Action Isn't Being Met," *ABA Banking Journal* 74 (October 13, 1983): 14.

7

MY LID DOTH FLIP—
BLACK MANAGERS
AND STRESS

In conceptualizing this research project, we were not aware of the nature and magnitude of the stress phenomenon black managers encountered in the banking industry. It was not until we got into the field with the open-ended personal interview schedule that we became aware of this problem.

We then sought to learn the sources of stress, as perceived by our respondents, to see how this stress affected them. In addition, we sought to learn what actions our respondents were taking to avoid, neutralize, or otherwise ameliorate the problems associated with stress.

We found that stress is serious and widespread among black managers and professionals, affecting both men and women adversely. We were encouraged, however, that not only were individuals beginning to take action to neutralize their job-related stress, but also local chapters of the NAUB are sponsoring seminars utilizing paid consultants to address the problem of stress.

One NAUB chapter approached this phenomenon on a highly sophisticated level. It sponsored seminars, charged professional fees, invited professional consultants, and made both tape cassettes and videos of the proceedings so that the results could be used repeatedly.

Others did similar things but perhaps on a less sophisticated level. It thus became clear to us that while stress is a significant problem, fortunately it is being recognized for what it is, and something is being done about it.

In this chapter we will try to analyze the problem of stress as perceived and experienced by black managers. In addition, we will briefly analyze the literature as it pertains to stress management.

This is not meant to be an exhaustive analysis, but rather an attempt to highlight the principle issues related to stress. The reader, then, is encouraged to pursue this subject further, in accordance with his interest. Accordingly, we have sought to include relevant bibliographic references for the guidance of the reader.

NO ONE ESCAPES STRESS

It has become a fact of life that everyone, black and white, male and female, young and old, is subject to stress. The sources of stress are almost as varied as human behavior itself. Black managers suffer from all the classical sources of stress. In addition, however, they encounter stress from racism. A fascinating, and still unresolved question is how much explanatory weight we should give to racism in our treatment of stress among black managers. If black managers do, in fact, experience a special kind of stress over and beyond the stress all other executives encounter in major corporations, how does this additional stress manifest itself and what can be done about it?

The testimony of many black managers whom we interviewed leaves little doubt that they are experiencing stress beyond that of their white peers. For example, one black male banker said:

> Just being black in the organization is a tension in itself. If I'm sitting with the other younger blacks in the organization, I sometimes notice a paranoia among them about being watched. You feel as though you're constantly being observed. Your actions are constantly being monitored. You constantly feel that you have to do over and above what is required. Then you feel as though that's not being evaluated fairly. Just the tension of going to meetings or calling on customers or going to bankers meetings and having 50 other bankers in the meeting and you're the only minority period.

For another black banker there was nothing figurative about the source of stress. For him the additional stress comes from white managers deliberately and routinely designing excessive workloads for him. Relating his experience, he said:

I recently received an assignment of . . . [bank] branches . . . that's double the normal workload, and the goal, as I am seeing and feeling it is: "Let's work him to death; let's give him plenty of things to do and hope that he makes some mistakes."

Obviously, not all stress experienced by black managers is derived from racism. For example, one senior black manager reported that his work had "a great deal" of stress associated with it mainly because, as he explained, "Managing a pretty sizeable portfolio is going to have an impact on the bank. So there is always tension associated with keeping your customer happy." This is obviously no different than would be true of any overworked employee. The only other major source of stress reported by this manager was the fact that his immediate supervisor was "a guy that is a very demanding individual on the one hand, and also an individual that is younger than I am and is clearly out for himself." The manager confessed, "I haven't built up, quite frankly, the trust relationship with him that I have with some other supervisors." Again there is nothing in this statement to differentiate the stress experienced by this black executive from that experienced by any other employee, black or white.

THE NATURE OF STRESS

There is a certain amount of confusion that exists regarding the causes of stress. Part of this confusion stems from the ambiguity in the concept of stress itself. The most cogent definition was offered years ago by Harry Levinson in his classic article, "What Killed Bob Lyons?" Stress, according to Levinson, is any threat to a person's effort to maintain psychological equilibrium between the person's need for status, recognition, esteem and the environment's demand. The threat produces a feeling of uneasiness or tension called anxiety, and this anxiety brings into play certain defense mechanisms (identification, repression, rationalization, displacement, and so on).[1] Confusion stems from the fact that the term *stress* is used to designate both the external threat and the internal chain of psychological reactions which ultimately defuse the threat.

Failure to draw such a distinction led stress theorists of the early 1960s to suggest, without qualification, that additional stress may be an asset.[2] These writers failed to consider that a point of internal diminishing return may be reached beyond which increased stress becomes counterproductive. Few would argue that stress-producing racism is an asset. More recent theories have compounded the confusion by advancing an essentially one-dimensional conception of stress.[3] Stress is simply a reflection of one's reaction to environmental factors — for example, feelings of competence and satisfaction with one's work. In this regard, one person may be totally upset with respect to his job situation, thus generating considerable stress. With the same scenario another person may be able to "roll with the punches," thereby generating very little stress. The difference in the stress generated in situations such as this is the attitude one brings to the situation, rather than the circumstances themselves.

Despite the continued confusion, experimental research and advances in psychoanalytic theories of stress dating back to the early 1900s have done much to decode the mystery of stress. In laboratory experiments conducted at the Harvard Physiologic Laboratory, Drs. Robert M. Yerkes and John D. Dodson were the first to demonstrate both the beneficial and damaging effects of stress. The inverted-U relationship which their experiments disclosed between stress, performance and efficiency, known as the Yerkes-Dodson law, states that as stress increases from a more or less zero-stress level, so do efficiency and performance. But if stress continues to increase beyond a given point, performance and efficiency begin to decrease.[4] Experiments by Dr. Walter B. Cannon of the Harvard Medical School advanced our understanding of stress still further by documenting the specific physiological changes — increased blood pressure and heart rate, sweating, faster breathing, and markedly increased blood flow to the muscles — which occur during stressful periods. These physiological changes, occurring in an integrated systematic pattern which Dr. Cannon called the "fight-or-flight response," were subsequently traced by Swiss Nobel Laureate, Dr. Walter R. Hess to a specific area of the brain called the hypothalamus and its release of adrenalin and noradrenalin. Hess's experiments (confined to cats) were substantiated by the investigations of Czech scientists, Dr. Jan Brod and his associates using human subjects in a laboratory setting.[5]

SOURCES OF STRESS

These experimental findings permit us to understand somewhat better the precise nature, if not the cause, of the additional stress black managers are experiencing. To illustrate this stress phenomenon as it affects black managers vis-à-vis their white peers, we have constructed a diagram (Exhibit 7.1).

Let us assume for the moment that black managers are bombarded with the same set of stresses as white managers and, as a consequence, are operating mainly in Region A, which is the left side of the inverted-U stress curve. Now suppose the set of internal and external stresses on black managers associated with working in a *white male-dominated racist* environment are added and persist

EXHIBIT 7.1
Yerkes-Dodson Stress/Performance Curve

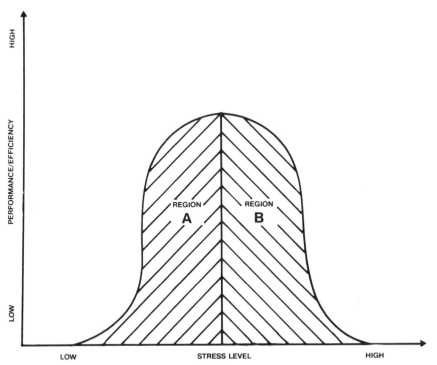

Source: Herbert Benson, "Your Innate Asset for Combating Stress," *Harvard Business Review*, July-August 1974, Vol. 52, pp. 49-60.

on a sustained, uninterrupted basis. According to Cannon, Hess, and others, this prolonged race-related stress will trigger a fight-or-flight response in black managers and shift them from Region A to Region B of the Yerkes-Dodson curve, where the damaging effects of prolonged excessive stress exist. These are measured specifically in terms of the chronic over activity of the hypothalamus (see Exhibit 7.1).

As set forth above, much of the stress which black managers face is not race specific.

The following exchange between a black female second vice-president and an interviewer illustrates the corporate-wide non-race specific stress black and white executives experience:

Female Second Vice-President (FSVP): I was hired for a job that never really came about. Then there was a change in management again. When my position was not clearly defined, I was under a lot of pressure, a lot of tension.

Interviewer: The ambiguity of your job is what gave you your source of tension.

FSVP: Yes, and once it became more clearly defined, we were reorganized again.

Interviewer: Are you saying that it is in the nature of the job, and it has nothing to do with black-white differences?

FSVP: I would think so.

Later during the interview, however, the manager also disclosed the special kind of stress reserved for blacks:

> The thing that creates tension for me, is being in an atmosphere of all whites who may say things . . . I don't particularly agree with [and whose jokes I don't find particularly funny] . . . . Being around whites all the time is an adjustment. And there are times when that's a tension kind of situation that I feel that I deal with just by pretending.

A black male executive from the East Coast made the same point:

> There is stress at being different and knowing that the reaction to your being different is always going to be there and it can't be masked. It's painful . . . I go through some of that whenever customers come in. They talk to me on the phone, and my voice hasn't given them an

indication that I am black. They walk in, you extend a hand, and all of a sudden, you hear them saying to themselves "You're not what I expected." . . . It's written all over their faces.

The kind of stress black managers are subjected to is quite subtle, as the following remarks by an executive of a major bank in the South illustrate. Referring to the constant tug-of-war with noncooperative white subordinates, the manager discussed one of his white male subordinates:

Many times . . . there are things that he [the white subordinate] does not want to do . . . so he will tell the customer, "You have to see the manager to get this done." Well [by now] the customer . . . has been to the teller's window, the teller has referred them to the white male, and then they get referred to me. To avoid shuffling the customer, again, I handle it. Later you tell your white male subordinate "Don't refer this type person to me anymore because here is what you can do to solve the problem."

The black manager had prefaced these remarks with a revelation that his white male subordinate already knew this and was routinely referring customers to him out of "laziness, or perhaps a more sinister motive."

Whatever the real reason for his subordinate's action, the fact that it was a persistent and chronic occurrence had become a source of stress for the black manager beyond the pressures any executive would normally encounter.

Another race-related source of stress stems from white subordinates who short-circuit the management chain of delegated authority and deliberately or unconsciously embarrass or dilute the organizational power of a black manager. The same black bank manager:

The guy in charge of all operations [my boss] . . . came out to discuss some operations problems left by the head teller with whom we had problems. . . . Some of them I was aware of, but others I did not know about at all. Obviously, somebody had been reporting around me instead of to me.

The black manager was especially agitated by the manner in which the problems were brought to his superior and the fact that his superior condoned this process. He continued:

Another lady came from another banking center to train a new head teller, and this lady . . . was old and was determined that everything must go her way. So she calls my boss, without discussing the matter with me. Here again, it's like a teller reporting to a regional manager regarding a branch manager and the regional manager listens to what the teller says without inquiring as to what the branch manager thought about this issue, or if he had been consulted.

The appropriate course would have been for my supervisor to raise the question: "Have you discussed this problem with your supervisor?" But since this was not done, it had the effect of diluting my control over my employees, and thus creating considerable stress for me.

NEUTRALIZING STRESS

What can be done to alleviate the additional stress black managers are being subjected to? Stated in terms of Exhibit 7.1, what can be done to shift the majority of black executives from Region B of the inverted-U stress curve where stress is destructive to Region A where stress and the fight-or-flight response have been found to increase efficiency and improve performance? Addressing the issue of excessive stress generally, Dr. Herbert Benson and his associates at the Harvard Medical School recommend a combination of regular exercise and the elicitation of the *relaxation response*.[6] Exercise — swimming, jogging, tennis, and so on — the traditional means, essentially involve burning off the physiological changes produced by the fight-or-flight response to stress.

Less well known in Western society until quite recently is the method of relaxation response. First described by Dr. Walter Hess, the Swiss Nobel Prize-winning physiologist, the response brings about physiological changes which are the precise opposite of those produced by the fight-or-flight response. "The overall metabolism of the body drops markedly," Dr. Benson notes, "heart and breathing rates decrease, blood flow to the muscles stabilizes, and blood pressure falls."[7]

In view of the above physiological reactions, Dr. Benson believes the conscious triggering of the relaxation response is ideally suited for reducing excessive stress. Describing the technique, Dr. Benson notes:[8]

The relaxation response is elicited by the use of age-old behavioral techniques, including Western relaxation methods, Eastern meditative practices, and certain types of prayer. The techniques contain four basic elements necessary to bring forth the response: a quiet environment; a comfortable position; the repetition of a word [for instance, the number *one*], phrase, or prayer; and the adoption of a passive attitude when other thoughts come into consciousness. The mind should be totally free of thoughts, free to just relax. Conscious thoughts should be driven out. Fifteen to twenty minutes of this exercise can totally relax one, lessen his blood pressure and slow his breathing. Practiced once or twice per day can totally rid one of body and emotional tensions.

Dr. Benson is convinced that the relaxation response is "therapeutically useful in diseases related to stress. . . . It has been established as an effective therapy for high blood pressure, many forms of irregular heartbeat, and symptoms associated with tension headaches and anxiety."[9]

Assuming its general applicability, the immediate question for black executives is whether the relaxation response technique will work for them. Several black managers in the interview group acknowledged their awareness [and use] of this technique. One black male manager disclosed his method for handling stress. "Earlier this year," he explained, "I got physically and emotionally ill, and so I sought professional advice." He recounted some of the techniques, "mental, physical, and I know that there are others but I can't think of the categories." Prompted by the interviewer, the executive mentioned exercise to "break down the tension." The manager then mentioned without elaborating "understanding yourself better and learning how to relax."

The black manager mentioned earlier in connection with the white female subordinate who circumvented lines of authority described how he resorted to the relaxation response to handle the kind of stress resulting from such incidents.

> The other employees really look to me for leadership and I know if I sit in there with a sad face or I look angry, it affects all of them. So what I do . . . [is] go in the back in the conference room, and I pray.

A black female executive on the West Coast disclosed: "I meditate every morning." Other more conventional stress-reduction techniques include exercise, reading, and playing cards. "I redirect every frustration that I have into a little thing called squash ball," a male executive from the West Coast noted. "The ball is about as hard as a rock and I can fire it at about 100 mph with the swing of my backhand, and I do."

Dr. Benson has listed a number of relaxation response techniques including transcendental meditation [TM], Zen and Yoga, autogenic training, progressive relaxation, hypnosis, and sentic cycles.[10] Table 7.1 compares the effect of the various relaxation response techniques. Again, however, we need to know how likely any one of these techniques is to effectively defuse the kind of stress black executives are experiencing. Is it really appropriate to recommend a technique which is based on the premise that nothing can be done about the source of excessive stress. Dr. Benson writes:

> It is unlikely that the rapid pace of Western life will slow down significantly; and as far as our present standard of living depends on that pace, it is unlikely that most executives would want it to slow down. The need for behavioral adjustment will probably continue; therefore, individuals should learn to counteract the harmful effects of the physiologic response to stress. One possibility is the regular elicitation of the relaxation response.[11]

Certainly such a prescription seems sensible for combatting excessive stress in general. But surely we are not about to suggest that nothing can be done about the source of the additional stress associated with racism, or that the only course of action left to black managers is to control their physiologic responses to stress. As a short-term technique, the relaxation response technique, coupled with regular exercise, may hold the key to black managers surviving the most damaging effects of prolonged race-connected stress. Over the long haul, stiffer, more system-wide medicine seems appropriate — medicine that conceivably would address, in social psychological terms, the environmental as well as internal sources of stress.[12]

We have purposely concentrated our analysis of the stress environment of black managers on the neutralization and treatment side of stress, on the thesis that these actions are in the control reach of black managers themselves. We make no pretense that our treatment is exhaustive. Current literature is filled with books and articles on stress. We have included a select number of stress publications in our bibliography.

TABLE 7.1
Techniques for Inducing the Relaxation Response

Technique	Physiologic Measurement					
	Oxygen Consumption	*Respiratory Rate*	*Heart Rate*	*Alpha Waves*	*Blood Pressures*	*Muscle Tension*
Transcendental meditation	Decreases	Decreases	Decreases	Increases	Decreases	Not measured
Zen and Yoga	Decreases	Decreases	Decreases	Increases	No change	Not measured
Autogenic training	Not measured	Decreases	Decreases	Increases	Inconclusive results	Decreases
Progressive relaxation	Not measured	Not measured	Not measured	Not measured	Inconclusive results	Decreases
Hypnosis with suggested deep relaxation	Decreases	Decreases	Decreases	Not measured	Inconclusive results	Not measured
Sentic cycles	Decreases	Decreases	Decreases	Not measured	Not measured	Not measured

Source: Herbert Benson, "Your Innate Asset for Combatting Stress," *Harvard Business Review*, July-August 1974.

AVOIDING STRESS

Obviously, the most fundamental solution to stress is to seek to get at the direct cause of the stress. *Under no condition should stress be ignored on the thesis that it will go away of its own volition.*

For example, if a subordinate, white or black, persists in circumventing a black manager as his superior, an acceptable approach would be to call the subordinate into the supervisor's office at a calm moment and suggest to the employee that he is violating organizational policy and should refrain from that type behavior. If it persists, write the employee a brief memo reminding him of the earlier admonishment. If it continues, a brief letter should be written to the supervisor, including a copy of the original memo to the subordinate. The disruptive nature of that behavior should be emphasized. You may be wise to "copy" your boss's supervisor and perhaps, Personnel. Keep the language unemotional and objective. The chances are this will stop this behavior.

There are always risks associated with any action to solve a problem, but it should be borne in mind that there are also risks associated with *no action*. Thus, the "action risk" must be seen as a trade-off with the "no action risk."

In this case the no action risk is likely to be diminished control of not only the subordinate, but more likely, of other employees. A subordinate over whom a supervisor has no control tends to become obvious to other subordinates in the department, thus radiating his behavior to them. In addition, such employees tend to do "their thing," not "your thing" for which you are being held responsible. With little or no control of one's employees, one is likely to be judged harshly by a superior for lack of productivity.

The action risk alternative entails possible alienation of one's supervisor who may be covertly encouraging the circumvention process. The documentation of this behavior is designed: (1) to alert your supervisor so that he becomes aware that you expect a reasonable structure within which to do your job; (2) that you know what that structure should be; and (3) that management at the next highest level is aware of the problem. In most cases, this approach should solve the problem and help one maintain self-respect.

However, if this approach gets you in irrevocable trouble, you didn't have a future there to begin with. You are wasting your time, postponing the inevitable. Consult your mentor, if you have one. If not, begin a search for a new job but keep low key until you get it. *Smile when you leave, and tell them it has been "real good" knowing and working with them as you walk out the door.*

RACISM AS A STRESS MEDIUM

We emphasize that racism (as a stress medium) is an American problem rather than a banking industry problem. However, as insidious as it is, it is likely to be a reality in the predictable future in our opinion.

The common problems can and should be understood and approached on two levels, that is, the individual and the organizational level.

Unfortunately, the nature of racism is that it frequently is interwoven into the fabric of the normal problems associated with organizational behavior without regard to race. While the demarcation line between normal organizational problems and racism cannot be definitively measured, the first step in one's effort to distinguish between the problems common to all organizations and racism is to first isolate those common problems. This, then, narrows the scope within which racism can be considered a factor.

The most important problems can be classified into two broad groups, that is, those which are individually imposed and those that are organizationally imposed. Examples of both are shown in Table 7.2. For best results, one is wise to concentrate upon those self-imposed sources of potential stress. These are likely to yield to success with the least amount of energy expenditure. Careful scrutiny of one's own weaknesses is the first step in the process of assessing racism.

Having ruled out one's self as the source of the problem, one can then assess the organizationally inspired problems. Even after pinpointing the source of the organizationally inspired problems, it is conceivable that the problem may stem, in part, from racism. Distinguishing between the fundamental problem and racism will be difficult and often impossible under some circumstances. However, this type analysis narrows the scope within which the issue of racism can be analyzed.

TABLE 7.2
Some Key Sources of Stress

Individually Imposed	*Organizationally Imposed*
• Lack of self-confidence	• Excessive work demands
• Poor communication skills	• Lack of feedback from supervisor
• Inappropriate dress habits	• Exclusion from informal network
• Unclear goals	• Responsibility without commensurate authority
• Unrealistic ambitions	• Unclear lines of authority and responsibility
• Substandard job performance	• Inadequate support systems to accomplish job
• Being perceived as noncooperative	• Condoning circumvention of lines of authority
• Inability to initiate relationships with peers and other associates	• Dead-end boss
• Inability to learn from one's mistakes	• Poor supervisor, in general
• Failure to evidence loyalty to supervisor and organization	• Underutilization of one's talents

One approach to the process of distinguishing between racism and the fundamental problem is to ask peers what their experience with the fundamental problem has been. Obviously, if most of one's peers perceive the problem to be fundamental, the likelihood of racism being the cause is nominal or maybe nonexistent. Thus the stress derived from one's misconception that the problem is racism is diminished.

Whether the problem is due to personal weaknesses, organizational behavior, or to racism, one's long-term future is best served by a rational and systematic effort to solve the problem. To ignore it is to exacerbate the problem and perhaps to stifle one's career.

In conclusion, we have tried to convey in this chapter that stress, up to a point, can be good. Beyond this point, however, stress is detrimental. Ignoring the signs of beneficial stress can lead to detrimental stress, later. Beneficial stress sends signals that one needs to improve or do something constructive. If it goes unheeded, the stress becomes negative and threatens sound physical and mental health. The alert person, then, will constantly evaluate and react to the signals radiated by stress, heeding what is beneficial and seeking to avoid or neutralize detrimental stress.

Such an approach will contribute to the maximization of one's potential while enhancing one's health, mentally and physically.

NOTES

1. Psychologist Harry Levinson provides an excellent overview of this process in his classic article, "What Killed Bob Lyons?" *Harvard Business Review*, March-April 1981, Vol. 59, No. 2, pp. 144-62.

2. See for example, David W. Ewing, "Tension Can Be an Asset," *Harvard Business Review*, September-October 1964, Vol. 42, No. 5, pp. 71-78.

3. In their otherwise excellent treatment of the disruptive emotional side effects of success, Bartolome and Evans advance an essentially one-dimensional theory of emotional spillover. According to this theory, the primary cause for the deterioration in the private lives of otherwise successful executives is to be found in work which "consistently produces negative feelings that overflow into private life." See Fernando Bartolome and Paul A. Lee Evans, "Must Success Cost So Much?" *Harvard Business Review*, March-April 1980, Vol. 58, No. 2, pp. 137-48.

4. See Robert M. Yerkes and John D. Dodson, "The Relation of Strength of Stimulus to Rapidity of Habit-Formation," *Journal of Comparative Neurology and Psychology*, 1908, p. 459.

5. For a review of the findings of Yerkes, Dodson, Cannon, and others see Herbert Benson, "Your Innate Asset for Combating Stress," *Harvard Business Review*, September-October 1980, Vol. 58, No. 5, pp. 86-92.

6. Benson and Allen, "Your Innate Asset," pp. 87-88.

7. Ibid., p. 88.

8. Ibid.

9. Ibid.

10. Ibid., p. 52.

11. Ibid.

12. See Levinson, "What Killed Bob Lyons?" for a remarkable synthesis of stress literature, and suggestions on how one might incorporate relaxation response techniques into a more comprehensive strategy.

8

THE WORK IS HARD—
WHAT'S THE PAY LIKE?

As pointed out earlier in this study, salary is not the most important factor with respect to job satisfaction of our respondents. Clearly, there is a salary level below which almost anyone would be unhappy with his job. This level is not a fixed amount but bears some relationship to how one compares with peers, given similar job responsibilities and qualifications.

In an effort to ascertain how our sample respondents compare with their peers in the banking industry in general, we have developed a table setting forth banking industry salaries by job title, age, length of service, and the number of years in the current position (see Table 8.1). In addition, we have developed an index of salaries of selected regions throughout the United States, using the national average as a base. The six regions which we selected represent the areas in which most of our sample respondents worked (see Table 8.2). By some standards, the salaries presented in Table 8.1 may be low, but it should be borne in mind that they are the base onto which bonuses and other emoluments available to the employee that would normally have to be paid from after-tax salary income by the employee are added. These "add-ons" vary so widely that it is difficult to generalize what the typical value of this indirect income is. Therefore, we have elected not to try to quantify that portion of the banking industry's salaries.

TABLE 8.1
Median Base Salary by Job Title, Age, Length of Service, Banks
$1 Billion in Assets and Above, 1983

Selected Job Titles	Salary	Age	Length of Service	Years in Position
Sr. Commercial Loan Officer	$ 38,692	42.0	10.0	4.5
Commercial Loan Officer	25,800	38.0	7.0	4.0
Sr. Consumer Loan Officer	28,000	43.0	11.0	5.0
Consumer Loan Officer	25,254	37.5	9.0	4.0
Sr. Mortgage Loan Officer	30,500	43.0	12.0	5.0
Mortgage Loan Officer	23,050	39.0	9.0	4.0
Trust Account Administrator	33,125	42.0	11.0	6.0
Corporate Trust Officer	29,500	40.0	10.0	5.0
Personal Trust Officer	29,909	43.0	10.5	5.0
Staff Attorney	35,333	37.0	4.5	3.5
Loan Review Officer	28,200	37.0	8.0	2.0
Personnel Assistant	15,337	37.0	6.0	3.0
Employment Interviewer	17,600	28.0	6.0	2.0
Assistant Branch Manager	23,685	41.0	12.0	3.0
Officer Trainee (BA)	14,765	25.0	2.0	1.0
Officer Trainee (MA)	23,376	27.5	1.5	1.0
Chief Executive Officer	200,000	50.0	14.0	7.0
Chief Administrator	132,004	46.0	12.0	5.0
Chief Financial Officer	70,000	43.0	9.5	4.0
Senior Operations Officer	57,000	42.0	12.0	5.0
Operations Officer	36,688	39.0	10.5	4.0
Personnel Officer/Director	58,000	42.0	10.0	4.0
Controller	52,500	39.0	9.0	4.0
General Accounting	32,800	38.5	11.0	4.0
Branch Administrative Officer	47,100	43.0	12.0	3.0
Branch Manager	26,801	42.0	11.0	4.0
Commercial Credit Department Manager	37,000	38.0	7.0	3.0
Consumer Loan Department Manager	43,000	43.0	11.0	4.5
Mortgage Loan Department Manager	50,400	44.0	13.0	4.5
Commercial Loan Department Manager	59,004	42.0	9.0	4.0
Senior Trust Officer	67,100	45.0	11.0	6.5
Trust Operations Manager	39,800	41.0	9.0	4.0
Sr. Business Development Officer	33,000	45.0	9.0	1.5
Sr. International Banking Officer	56,000	45.0	8.0	4.5
Sr. Investment Officer	67,000	42.0	12.0	5.0

Source: 1983 BAI Bank Officer Cash Compensation Survey.

TABLE 8.2
Index of Median Base Salary by Job Title and Region, Banks $1 Billion in Assets and Above, 1983

Selected Job Titles	($000)	National Region					
		I	II	III	IV	V	VI
Sr. Commercial Loan Officer	38.6	.96	.87	.86	1.13	.88	.90
Commercial Loan Officer	26.0	1.04	.97	.93	.92	.91	.98
Sr. Consumer Loan Officer	28.0	.93	.83	.93	1.49	1.02	1.02
Consumer Loan Officer	25.2	.61	1.19	.85	.91	.87	.93
Sr. Mortgage Loan Officer	31.0	.97	.83	1.11	1.00	.93	1.12
Mortgage Loan Officer	23.3	.87	.94	.85	1.12	.81	.82
Trust Account Administrator	29.0	.60	1.00	.82	*	*	*
Corporate Trust Officer	28.3	*	*	*	1.17	1.02	1.04
Personal Trust Officer	15.3	*	.89	.84	1.11	*	*
Staff Attorney	18.0	*	1.14	1.02	1.00	*	1.10
Loan Review Officer	28.2	*	1.06	*	*	*	*
Personnel Assistant	15.3	.92	.91	.88	1.00	.86	.88
Employment Interviewer	17.6	*	.91	.98	1.03	*	1.13
Assistant Branch Manager	24.0	*	.84	1.09	.99	.68	*
Officer Trainee (BA)	15.0	.95	1.00	.91	.99	.83	.98
Officer Trainee (MA)	23.3	*	*	*	*	*	*
Chief Executive Officer	200.0	*	.86	1.13	*	*	*
Chief Administrator	138.0	*	.99	1.00	*	*	*
Chief Financial Officer	70.0	*	1.04	*	1.43	*	*
Sr. Operations Officer	57.0	*	.84	*	*	*	*

	National	I	II	III	IV	V	VI
Operations Officer	36.7	*	1.01	*	.95	*	*
Personnel Officer/Director	58.0	*	1.00	*	1.21	*	*
Controller	52.5	*	.95	*	1.08	*	*
General Accounting	33.0	*	*	*	1.16	*	*
Branch Administrative Officer	47.1	*	1.00	*	*	*	*
Branch Manager	27.0	*	.99	.90	.92	*	*
Commercial Credit Department Manager	37.0	*	*	*	1.08	*	*
Consumer Loan Department	43.0	*	.96	*	.99	*	*
Mortgage Loan Department Manager	50.4	*	.96	*	1.30	*	*
Commercial Loan Department Manager	59.0	*	*	*	1.15	*	*
Sr. Trust Officer	67.1	*	*	*	1.44	*	*
Trust Operations Manager	40.0	*	*	*	1.24	*	*
Sr. Business Development Officer	33.0	1.09	1.00	1.21	1.12	1.05	1.00
Sr. International Banking Officer	56.0	*	*	*	*	*	*
Sr. Investment Officer	67.0	*	.93	1.03	1.04	.96	*

Note: National salaries have been rounded.

*Indicates insufficient data, median base salary of all banks used.

Region I – New England: Connecticut, Maine, Massachusetts, New Hampshire, Rhode Island, Vermont.

Region II – Mid Atlantic: New Jersey, New York, Pennsylvania.

Region III – South Atlantic: Delaware, Florida, Georgia, Maryland, North Carolina, South Carolina, Virginia, Washington, D.C., West Virginia.

Region IV – East-North Central: Illinois, Indiana, Michigan, Ohio, Wisconsin.

Region V – West-South Central: Arkansas, Louisiana, Oklahoma, Texas.

Region VI – Pacific: Alaska, California, Hawaii, Oregon, Washington.

Source: 1983 BAI Bank Officer Cash Compensation Survey.

SALARIES – THE INDUSTRY FRAMEWORK

The salaries set forth in Table 8.1 represent 35 job titles selected from a set of 96 that are common in the banking industry. These 35 titles bear some relationship to the types of jobs which our sample respondents either occupy currently, or to higher jobs in the line of their career progression. These salaries were collected by the Bank Administration Institute, an arm of the American Bankers Association which conducts research in the "Operations Function" of the industry. The Operations Function covers internal management functions other than lending and investments. The 1983 survey, from which these data were extracted, was the eighth annual survey conducted on bank salaries by the institute.[1] The tables are self-explanatory; however, we thought it would be instructive to highlight a few of the titles that were most prevalent among our sample.

From Table 8.1 it can be seen that a senior commercial loan officer earned a base salary of $36,000 annually, and was 42 years old. He had been with his bank for ten years and in his present position for 4½ years. A senior mortgage officer earned an average of $31,000 annually. He was 38 years old, with nine years of tenure with the firm and four years in his present position. (For information regarding numerous other jobs, see Table 8.1.)

REGIONAL DIFFERENCES IN BANK SALARIES

In an effort to provide information on regional differences in salaries, we developed a chart which indexed the regions to the national averages. The regions listed are those within which most of our respondents work. Thus, with the national average representing 100, each region was computed as a ratio to that base. For example, it can be seen in Table 8.2 that a senior operations officer earned a base salary of $57,000 on a national average. In all but one of the six regions the salaries earned for this position were below the national average. Other job titles can be analyzed similarly.

SALARIES OF SAMPLE RESPONDENTS

With the industry salaries on a national and regional level as a frame of reference, we felt it would be useful to examine the salary profile of our respondents in this context. The average salary for men in our sample was $35,000, while women earned an average of $25,630. Forty percent of the men fell in the $30,000 to $45,000 range. Significantly, approximately 16 percent of the male bankers earned salaries in excess of $50,000, while only 2 percent of females earned over $50,000 (see Exhibit 8.1).

The reasons for the wide disparity between black male and black females are similar to those that prevail for the U.S. population in general. This issue is analyzed in some depth in a later section of this chapter.

In an effort to gain more definitive insight into the dynamics of salary income of blacks in the banking industry, we analyzed the salaries of our sample respondents in relation to six variables. They are age, education, tenure in the industry, tenure in the bank where they currently work, job function, and job title.

SALARIES – EDUCATION AND SEX

As can be seen in Exhibit 8.2 there is a high correlation between salary and education among our sample respondents. For example, while the weighted average of salary for men was $34,200 annually, it is significant that male MBAs earned an average of $38,600, or a salary 46 percent higher than that of bankers with only high school education. Similarly, while women earned an average of $25,850 annually, female MBAs earned 53 percent more than female bankers with high school education.

As set forth above, black men earned 32 percent higher salaries than black women in the banking industry. This disparity may be attributable to two main causes. Perhaps the most important one is the higher education level of men. In this regard, from Exhibit 8.2 it can be seen that 26 percent of the men fell into the category of having had "high school or some college education," while almost twice as many women, or 46 percent, fell within these two classes. Similarly, men held three times as many MBAs as women, that is, 26 percent versus 8 percent, respectively.

Another way of gaining insight into the disparity in education and earnings levels between black men and black women in the banking industry is to examine the relative position each sex occupies in key educational levels. For example, in our sample black women comprised 67 percent of all bankers with high school education.

EXHIBIT 8.1
Base Salaries of Sample Bankers, by Sex

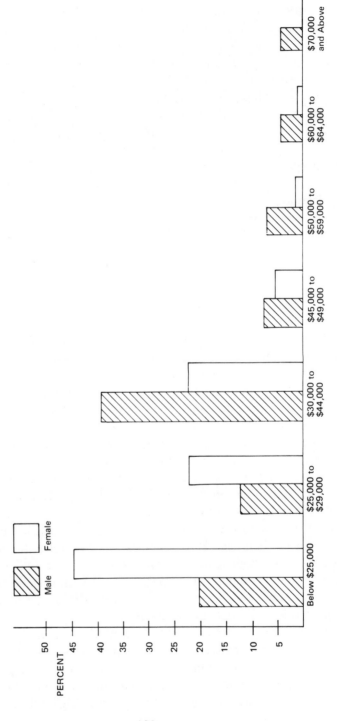

EXHIBIT 8.2
Median Base Salary by Education and Sex ($000)

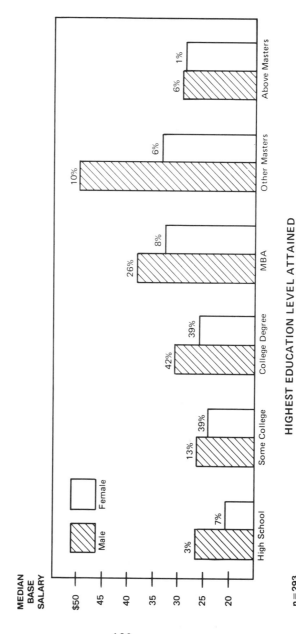

HIGHEST EDUCATION LEVEL ATTAINED

n = 293

NOTE: The percentage shown at the top of each bar reflects the percentage of each sex in the education level interval.

103

On the other hand, black men comprised almost eight out of ten MBAs in our sample. Men also represented six out of ten other masters degrees and nine out of ten other degrees above the masters. These data suggest that the higher salary of black men over black women appears to be based upon their educational achievement (Exhibit 8.2). The second but more subjective reason may have something to do with the widely held perception among our sample interviewees that black women tend to be less aggressive in pursuit of their careers than black men. This issue will be treated in more depth in Chapter 9.

SALARIES – AGE AND SEX

Our national data do not permit comparison of age with our sample respondents. While not as dramatically related as is education, age and salary are generally positively correlated. The correlation is not continuous throughout the total age spectrum, however. At this stage of black development on the management level in the banking industry, there appears to be a peak in the salary at the age of about 40 years, following which the salary level declines.

In Exhibit 8.3, for example, the average earning for men below the age of 30 was about $24,000, while the average was $45,000 for men between 30 and 40 years of age. Above 40 years of age, the average for men declined to $41,250. The pattern for women was similar, but at a lower level. In this regard, the average annual earning for women below 30 years of age was $25,000, while their earnings were $34,800 between 30 and 40 years of age. Their annual salary dropped to $26,900 above the age of 40.

This phenomenon is counter to the age-salary cohort behavior of the population in general. In general, earnings of most Americans gradually reach a peak and remain there until retirement. Barring major economic upheavals, they do not generally fall before retirement.

From the data available, one cannot be certain as to the cause of this salary behavior among black Americans in the banking industry. A reasonable postulate is that while they were younger, the older persons in the industry were given titles with only nominal salaries while the more recent hires with higher education were being brought into the industry with higher salaries. This appears

EXHIBIT 8.3
Median Salary by Age and Sex ($000)

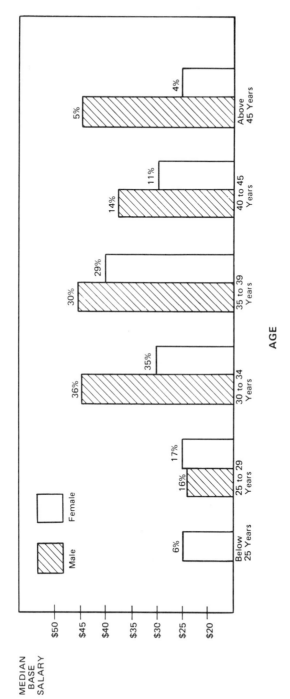

NOTE: The percentage shown at the top of each bar reflects the percentage of each sex in the age interval.

to be more pronounced among the female bankers than among males. For example, the average salary of black women over 40 dropped 22 percent below their average salary between 30 and 40 years old. On the other hand, men's salaries dropped only 8 percent over the same age span.

As can be seen in Exhibit 8.3, the average age of black Americans in our sample was 35 and 34 years for males and females respectively. It would not be meaningful to compare this average age with the average age of all of the job categories shown in Table 8.1. However, a cursory perusal of the various job categories in that table suggests that black Americans in the industry are about seven or eight years younger than those in the banking industry in general. This is not surprising, given the relatively short length of time that black Americans have been in the industry at the management level. It is also clear that while black Americans have not yet reached the upper middle management levels of the industry in significant numbers, their salaries for their present assignments appear to be competitive with those of their counterparts in the industry.

Finally, in spite of great similarity in the average age of black males and females in the banking industry, men earned approximately 29 percent more than females, $41,300 versus $31,900. This suggests that age is not the prime criterion for salary determination.

SALARIES AND TENURE IN THE INDUSTRY BY SEX

Tenure in the industry exerts considerable impact upon salaries. This impact is more pronounced for black males than for black females. For example, black male bankers who have been in the industry five years or more earn $57,500, or 48 percent more than those who have been in less than five years. For black women, the comparable increase is 25 percent (see Exhibit 8.4). The disparity could be the result of the extensively documented classical discrimination of women in the labor force with respect to earnings. It could also be the last vestige of the industry practice of relegating women to traditionally lower paying jobs. More definitive analysis of this issue would require more specific data than are inherent in this study. As in the case of age, the data do not permit comparative analysis of our sample and national data on tenure.

EXHIBIT 8.4

Median Base Salary by Tenure in Banking Industry and Sex ($000)

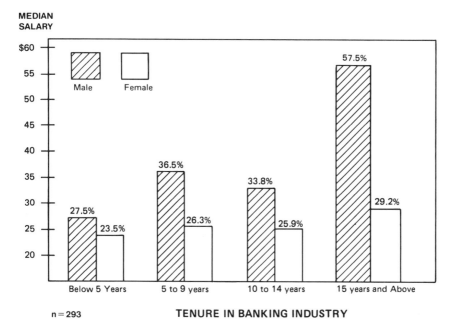

n = 293   **TENURE IN BANKING INDUSTRY**

NOTE: The percentage shown at the top of each bar reflects
        the percentage of each sex in the tenure interval

SALARIES AND TENURE IN CURRENT BANK BY SEX

Like tenure in the industry, tenure in the current bank is positively correlated with salary. As was true with the industry, men
experienced the largest salary increase as their tenure increased. For
example, those men whose tenure exceeded 15 years earned almost
49 percent higher salaries than those whose tenure was below five
years (see Exhibit 8.5). The comparable increase in salary for black
women was 17 percent. This is further evidence of sexism in the
industry. As for absolute salaries, black men earned $36,300 on
an average, or 42 percent higher than the $25,500 earned by black
women when weighted with respect to their tenure in their current
bank (Exhibit 8.5).

EXHIBIT 8.5

Median Base Salary by Tenure in Current Bank, by Sex ($000)

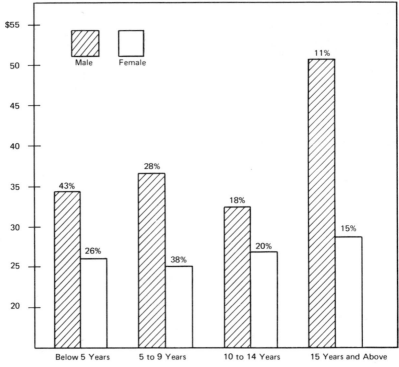

NOTE: The percentage shown at the top of each bar reflects
the percentage of each sex in the tenure interval

SALARIES BY JOB FUNCTION AND SEX

Not surprisingly, job function clearly makes a difference as
to what one can expect to earn in the banking industry. Commercial lending appears to be the highest paying function as represented
by our respondents. In this category or job classification, males
dominated the commercial lending function among our respondents
at a median salary of $37,800 (see Exhibit 8.6). This was 15 percent
higher than the $32,869 which black female commercial bankers

EXHIBIT 8.6
Median Base Salary by Job Function and Sex ($000)

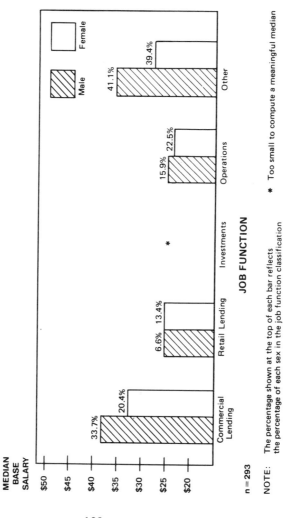

n = 293

NOTE: The percentage shown at the top of each bar reflects the percentage of each sex in the job function classification

* Too small to compute a meaningful median

109

earned. This salary disparity between black males and black females could result from one of two causes: (1) classical sexism which relegates women to lower salaries even for the same job function, or (2) a shorter tenure by females in commercial lending than their male counterparts (Exhibit 8.6). It is equally significant that the salary of black males compared favorably with the salary for senior commercial loan officers; black females also compare favorably, if we assume that they are not senior commercial loan officers. Our personal interviews suggest that this is a reasonable assumption. Both black males and females earn median salaries slightly above industry averages for senior commercial loan officer and commercial loan officer. It is significant that males occupied 71 percent of the higher paying commercial lending jobs among our respondents.

On the other hand, retail lending, the lower paying job, was dominated by women. They occupied 66 percent of these jobs. The average salary for both men and women was in the area of $25,000, 51 percent less than that of male commercial bankers and 32 percent less than that of female commercial bankers (Exhibit 8.6). This salary was also somewhat lower than the $31,000 median salary for consumer loan officers in the industry.

SALARIES BY JOB RANK AND SEX

Not surprisingly, salary increase comes with higher job rank. In this regard, male bankers among our respondents earned $30,000 at the "banking officer or below" job function and up to $70,000 and above for the "senior vice-president" level. Women, on the other hand, ranged from approximately $25,000 to approximately $46,000 (see Exhibit 8.7). Significantly, at the low end of the job category women occupied 63 percent of the jobs while at the "vice-president" level, men represented almost nine out of ten jobs.

SALARY IN PERSPECTIVE

The above analysis demonstrates clearly that black men have an overall higher education level than black women in the banking industry. They rank higher in the bank hierarchy and enjoy concomitantly higher salaries.

EXHIBIT 8.7
Median Base Salary by Job Rank and Sex ($000)

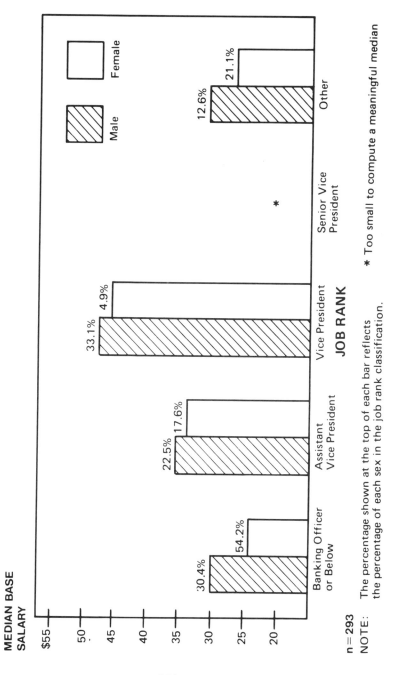

MEDIAN BASE
SALARY

Female

Male

$55
50
45
40
35
30
25
20

54.2%
30.4%

Banking Officer
or Below

22.5%
17.6%

Assistant
Vice President

33.1%
4.9%

Vice President

JOB RANK

*

Senior Vice
President

12.6%
21.1%

Other

* Too small to compute a meaningful median

n = 293

NOTE: The percentage shown at the top of each bar reflects
the percentage of each sex in the job rank classification.

Our research also suggests that while black Americans have yet to break through to upper-middle and top management functions to any measurable degree, they appear to be paid competitively with their white peers in the industry at the current job levels. The problem appears to be in the job ceilings placed upon minorities.

Our personal interviews revealed, however, that there is considerable resistance within the industry to the elevation of black Americans beyond the level of vice-president. What happens is that as soon as a black employee, especially a black male, reaches a point at which he would likely be a candidate for promotion beyond the vice-president level, the "system" sets in motion a confluence of forces apparently designed to make the candidate unhappy to the point where he will voluntarily leave, or to provoke him to the point that he will be fired.

For example, a male banker with a Midwest regional bank, who had recently earned his MBA after a number of years of working full time and going to school part time made this statement:

> They've given me no consideration since I've received my MBA. They still want me to run this small branch. So I'm looking around for a job outside the industry. I, personally, know of eight other black males in this town who've left the industry in 1983 for the same reasons. It's clear to us that they'd rather see us go than promote us. They then start the cycle over again from the bottom. The bottom line is they churn us at the bottom, without changing the relative numbers. We show up as a given level of statistics rather than human beings being crushed one by one.

By contrast, a young black female banker who had just earned her MBA in a similar manner made this statement when asked if she had received any additional recognition for having earned her MBA: "No I didn't. But then I didn't expect it. My MBA is not needed in the job which I currently have. So I went right on doing my job as before."

This point of view was supported by another female banker in a money center bank who, when asked if she planned to pursue the MBA responded: "I'm not leaning in that direction. I'm not sure it's worth the effort for me. I think I can get whatever this bank has to offer me without the wear and tear required to earn an MBA."

The contrasting attitudes of black males regarding the value of an MBA provides some evidence of the difference in expectations of black males and black females with respect to career movement. (It also gives credence to the notion articulated by our personal interviewees that white male supervisors tend to be more comfortable with black females than with black males.)

Finally, with respect to salaries earned by our respondents, the reader is reminded that our respondents ranked salary fifth in order of importance with respect to job satisfaction. This ranking agrees with employees in American industry generally as evidenced by prior research. Thus, like professionals and managers in general, black bank managers want to be paid salaries commensurate with their education, experience, and productivity, and competitively with their white peers. Under these conditions, the absolute amount of salary takes on less significance than most other factors affecting their careers.

NOTE

1. Andrew M. Mosko, *1983 BAI Bank Officer Cash Compensation Survey* (Rolling Meadows, Ill.: Bank Administration Institute, 1983).

9

WHAT'S WRONG WITH BLACK MEN?

There has been considerable debate in recent years regarding the improvement, or the lack thereof, of black Americans in employment relative to the general population since the Civil Rights Act of 1964. For example, in two landmark studies published in 1973, Professor Richard Freeman of Harvard University reported that there had been "a collapse in the economic differences separating black and white women," a "noticeable" improvement in the occupation of black males, especially highly skilled and college trained men, and a dramatic improvement in the rate of return of schooling to blacks (Freeman 1973a, 1973b).

If Professor Freeman's conclusions are representative of the country in aggregate, a clearly debatable point, they are less indicative of what is happening in the banking industry. In this regard, we examined the position of black Americans in the banking industry generally in Chapter 2. In this chapter, we will examine the impact of the banking industry's interpretation of the 1964 Civil Rights Act upon black Americans, particularly following the amendment of the Act in 1972 and the issuance of the guidelines affecting women by E.E.O.C. in 1972.

Since the mid-1960s, the number of employees in managerial, professional, and technician functions in the banking industry has grown significantly. In 1966 there were 98,228 employees in these three functions. By the end of 1981 there were 366,957 persons occupying these functions in the industry, almost quadruple the earlier period.

114

The impact of this growth upon black bankers was uneven. Before the 1964 Civil Rights Act, the industry had systematically excluded black Americans from all but the most menial tasks in the industry. By the end of the 15-year period ending in 1981, black women had reached 8.8 percent of the white collar employees of the industry, while black men made up only 2.6 percent of that employee group. This compared to 2 and 1 percent, respectively, for these two groups in 1966. The industry thus afforded black women significantly more employment opportunities than it did black men (see Table 9.1).

With respect to blacks in the management function, by the end of 1981 black females had reached the 2.4 percentage level of management jobs in the industry while black men represented only 1.9 percent. At this rate of growth, it would take approximately 25 years for black women to reach a management level commensurate with their general population ratio. It would take almost 40 years for black men to reach their population ratio. This assumes the current population of 6 and 5 percent respectively for black women and men will continue to prevail in the future.

THE GROWTH IN JOBS – WHO GOT THEM?

Additional insight may be gleaned from examining the growth dynamics of blacks in the industry and how that growth was shared by race and sex during the 15-year period ending in 1981. Of the 642,886 additional white collar employees added to the industry rolls during the 15-year period ending in 1981, white women were awarded the largest share, or 45 percent. White males received 30 percent of these jobs, followed by black females at 8.7 percent. Black males were awarded only 4 percent of the increase in white collar jobs during this period (see Table 9.2). With respect to the decision making, or the management and professional type job, white males and females were each awarded about the same percentage of these jobs, or 42 and 43 percent respectively, for a total of 86 percent. Black females, on the other hand, received only 4.0 percent, while black males, following the industry pattern cited above, received only 3 percent (Table 9.2).

TABLE 9.1
Percentage Share in Selected Banking Labor Force by Race and Sex — 1966 and 1981

Sector	1966					1981				
	Total*	W.M.	W.F.	B.M.	B.F.	Total*	W.M.	W.F.	B.M.	B.F.
Management	84,797	75,095	7,934	257	74	257,176	149,083	82,819	4,923	6,226
Percent	100	89.0	9.4	0.3	0.1	100	58.0	32.2	1.9	2.4
Professional	9,948	8,270	1,378	67	12	78,849	36,367	31,532	2,237	3,242
Percent	100	83.1	13.9	0.7	0.1	100	46.1	40.0	2.8	4.1
Technicians	3,483	2,046	1,044	66	167	30,932	13,843	10,228	2,170	1,899
Percent	100	58.7	30.0	1.9	4.8	100	44.8	33.1	7.0	6.8
Other White Collar	355,611	82,837	245,490	3,609	9,233	729,828	69,391	483,750	18,641	85,694
Percent	100	23.3	69.0	1.0	2.6	100	9.5	66.1	2.6	22.7
Total	453,839	170,498	255,602	3,999	9,486	1,196,785	268,689	608,329	27,971	97,061
Percent	100	37.6	56.3	.9	2.1	100	24.5	55.5	2.6	8.8

1966 – 1609 banks reporting; 1981 – 3072 banks reporting.
*Includes other groups as well as **WM, WF, BM** and **BL**: totals do not add to 100 percent.

Source: E.E.O.C. Annual Report, 1966 and 1981.

TABLE 9.2
Increase in Banking Labor Force Sectors, 1966-81

Sector	Absolute					Percentage Share				
	Total	W.M.	W.F.	B.M.	B.F.	Total	W.M.	W.F.	B.M.	B.F.
Management	172,379	73,988	74,885	4,666	6,152	100	42.9	43.4	2.7	3.6
Professional	68,901	28,097	30,154	2,170	3,230	100	40.8	43.8	3.1	4.7
Technicians	27,449	11,797	9,184	2,104	1,732	100	42.3	32.5	7.7	6.3
Subtotal	268,729	113,882	114,223	8,940	11,114	100	42.0	43.0	3.0	4.0
Other White Collar	347,217	(15,446)	238,260	15,032	76,461	100	(4.1)	63.7	4.0	20.4
Total	642,946	98,436	352,483	23,972	87,575	100*	30.4*	45.0*	4.4*	8.7*

1966 — 1609 banks reporting; 1981 — 3072 banks reporting.
*Mean of the percentages.

Source: E.E.O.C. Annual Report, 1966 and 1981.

BLACK BANKERS QUESTION E.E.O.C. STATISTICS

Given the E.E.O.C. statistics showing that black women appear to be selected and retained by the industry in preference to black men, we did two things to gain insight into the dynamics of this phenomenon. First we dichotomized the survey sample by sex and ran the satisfaction indexes to see if there were any differences between the level of satisfaction of black men versus black women. Secondly, we sought to find out from our personal interviews what was behind the apparent difference which the industry appeared to be making between black men and black women.

In reviewing the satisfaction indexes by sex, we were somewhat bewildered to discover that, utilizing the Spearman rank-order correlation technique, there were no discernible differences between the indexes of black men and black women. We thought black men would be more negative with respect to the industry, given what is happening to them in the industry, but this was not borne out by the satisfaction indexes. Only after we began our field interviews did we begin to see that while black women are being hired and retained at a greater rate than black men, their problems were similar to those of black men, varying only in degree.

WHY BLACK MEN LEAVE THE INDUSTRY

The difference appears to be in the reaction of black women versus black men to their negative environment. As one female banker in a Midwest regional bank stated:

> Black women are faced with the same crap that black men face. . . . But black men compare themselves to white men in the industry and they get tired of taking the s--- and leave. Black women, on the other hand, hang on hoping that things will finally get better. Unfortunately, they don't seem to, though. Maybe one here and there breaks through and gets an important job, but most of us just hang in there.

Similarly, when we asked our interviewees what was causing more black women to be elevated to more management positions than black men, we encountered negative responses from both men and women alike. Both felt that the E.E.O.C. statistics showing more women in management were misconstruing the facts. They indicated that black women, with few exceptions, are relegated to low-level operations supervisor jobs and small branch management functions, neither of which carry much weight in the total scheme of things. Black women, they feel, are more underutilized than black men. It will be recalled that the lion's share of jobs assigned to black women during the 15-year period ending 1981 were clerical (Table 9.2).

They felt that the E.E.O.C. statistics should be more refined so that low-level supervisory jobs could be distinguished from decision-making management jobs which have greater impact on the bank's direction and bottom line.

As one black male vice-president put it:

The industry is witnessing the entry of some very independent, very aggressive black females who now have the ticket. They come out [of school] with MBAs in finance and technical undergraduate degrees and they are able to deal head-on, one on one.

As another black male banker put it,

Part of the reason that more black women than black men are coming into the industry has to do with the "two-for" system, they fill two E.E.O.C. requirements for the price of one person. And secondly, white males in power seem to find it easier to deal with black females than black males.

That observation was confirmed by another black woman vice-president of a Midwestern regional bank. "White managers," she noted, "seem to think that they can handle a black female easier than they can a black man."

WHERE DOES IT LEAD?

From the above, it is obvious that the industry is following a policy of opting for women over men in general, and in particular, black women over black men. This practice began shortly after the guideline covering E.E.O.C. policies related to sex discrimination was issued in 1972. Thus, the trend line for hiring and retaining black men and women in the banking industry changed significantly after

1972. To assess the impact of this trend line on the future employment prospects of black men and women in the industry, we conducted a least squares trend analysis of each of the major white collar job functions, that is, management, professionals, technicians, and other white collar (mostly clerical functions).

We then extrapolated the trend which covered the 1974-81 period. Ideally, we would like to have a longer time period within which to conduct the trend analysis. A longer time frame would improve the validity of our extrapolation. The importance of the trend underway, however, does not lend itself to waiting another ten years before the analysis begins. We, therefore, opted to go with what we have. While it is possible that our extrapolations can be questioned because of the relatively short base period, it is significant that for six out of eight cases, the coefficient of correlation was above .90, ranging up to .99 and the standard errors were small (see Appendix to this chapter).

Obviously, no one can predict what the industry will, in fact, do in this regard or what the environment will be. The industry may or may not change the total or the mix of black male and female hirings in the future. If it does not, however, the percentage of black males and females in the various white collar functions will be as depicted on the four Exhibits 9.1A through 9.2B.

In Exhibit 9.1A, it can be seen that by 1990, 25 years after the Civil Rights Act of 1965 was passed, neither black men nor women will have acquired their share of management jobs in the banking industry in relationship to their general population ratio. Black women will have acquired only 4.4 percent of management jobs and that amount is 75 percent higher than that of black men. *It is significant that the industry has relegated black males to a no growth curve in three of the four white collar functions.* It is equally striking that black females surpassed black males for the first time in the history of the industry in 1977 in the management and professional job categories. They will surpass black males in the technicians category by 1985, if present industry hiring policies continue to prevail. By 1990, they will occupy 11.5 percent of the technicians jobs, about 35 percent higher than black males (Exhibit 9.2A).

With respect to the clerical function, black females have always outnumbered black males and if current hiring patterns persist, by 1990 they will occupy 16.5 percent of the clerical jobs, almost five times as many as black males.

EXHIBIT 9.1A
Black Managers: Linear Trend (1974-1981) and Extrapolation to 1990

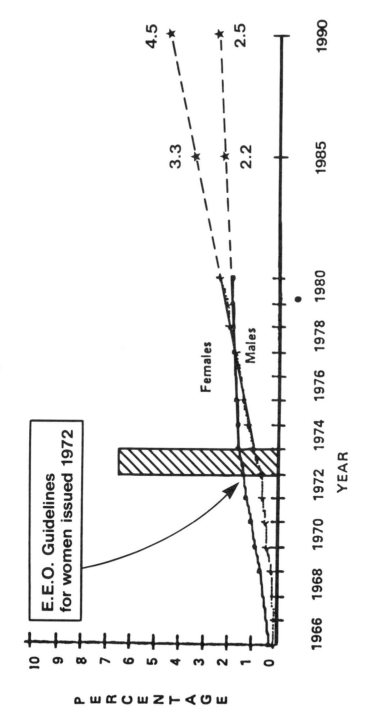

Source: E.E.O.C. Annual Reports, 1966-1981.

121

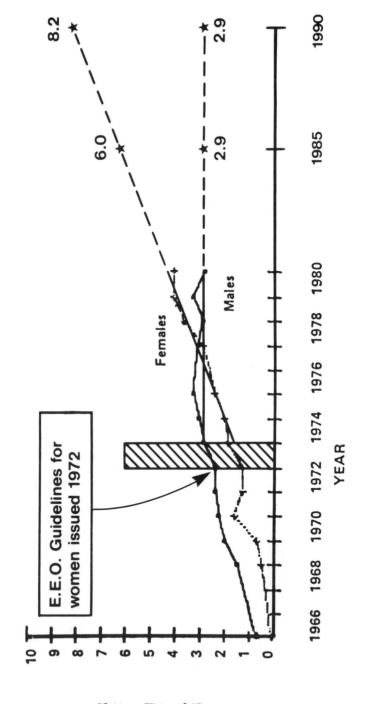

EXHIBIT 9.1B
Black Professionals: Linear Trend (1974–1981) and Extrapolation to 1990

Source: E.E.O.C. Annual Reports, 1966-1981.

122

EXHIBIT 9.2A
Black Technicians: Linear Trend (1974-1981) and Extrapolation to 1990

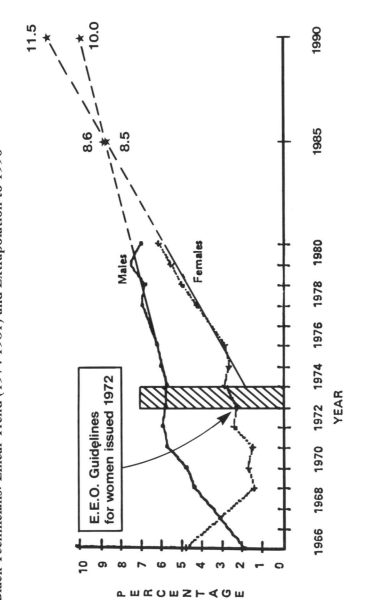

Source: E.E.O.C. Annual Reports, 1966-1981.

EXHIBIT 9.2B
Black Clerical Workers: Linear Trend (1974-1981) and Extrapolation to 1990

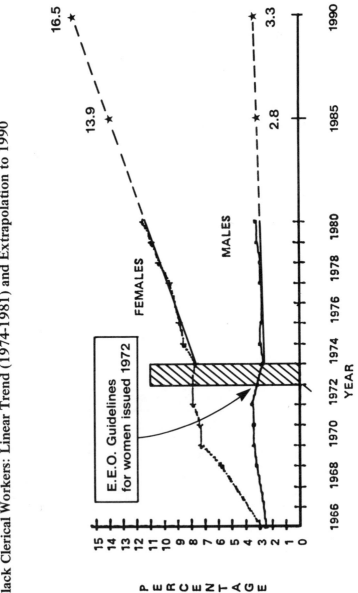

Source: E.E.O.C. Annual Reports, 1966-1981.

124

Finally, if industry leaders are using E.E.O.C. guidelines to govern their hiring practices of black men and women, either these guidelines need to be reinterpreted, or they need to be rewritten. It seems hardly plausible that Congress intended its civil rights laws to be used to screen black males out of the banking industry, or that black females be relegated to largely clerical and low level supervisory and staff functions, which appears to be happening at this point in history.

APPENDIX

Time Series Regression of Series of Shares of Banking Functions by Race and Sex

	Constant	*Slope*	R^2
Males			
Managers	1.52857	.060714	.90
	(.0397732)	(8.89356E-03)	
Professionals	3.1	−.0107147	.01
Technicians	5.48572	.285713	.89
	(.195861)	(.0437959)	
Others	1.95714	.0714283	.60
Females			
Managers	.742858	2.35714	.99
	(.0428608)	(9.58397E-03)	
Professionals	1.28572	.432142	.95
	(.192595)	(.0430656)	
Technicians	1.81429	.607142	.95
	(.281761)	(.060037)	
Others	7.95715	.532141	.91
	(.329388)	(.0736534)	

The regression formula utilized to generate coefficients was the least squares linear model $y = a + bx$.

Note: The numbers in parentheses represent the standard error.

10

THE HAND WRITES
ON THE WALL . . .
AND HAVING WRITTEN,
MOVES ON

By now, the reader must be convinced that the findings in this research project are the result of extensive and comprehensive statistical and qualitative analysis of the perceptions of black American managers/professionals in the banking industry. The reader is reminded that perceptions may or may not be based upon facts or reality. Nonetheless, the hand of history writes just as indelibly when perceptions are involved, whether those perceptions are based upon reality or upon illusions. Accordingly, the implications of those perceptions are just as real, regardless of whether they are based on facts or on fiction. The *stifling* or *destruction* of careers, the *cost* of recruiting and training personnel repetitiously, the *consumption* of management time and resources do not lessen because the perceptions may be based on illusions instead of reality.

In view of the above, the authors feel constrained to assert that as sensitive observers of the U.S. social scene, we were superficially aware of some of the problems uncovered by our research; however, we were not prepared for the magnitude and pervasiveness of the problems encountered by black and other minority Americans seeking to develop careers in the banking industry.

In this chapter we will set forth our summary and conclusions of this study. While as black Americans we were struck by the nature and breadth of the problems uncovered in it, as scholars we have sought scrupulously to avoid injecting our emotions into the analysis. Instead, we have attempted to let the facts speak for themselves, both in the recording of the data as well as in our analysis and interpretation of them.

Black Americans functioning on a white collar level constituted 4.3 percent of the banking industry in 1982. While this was an increase relative to the percentage they occupied in the industry 20 years earlier, it is still only one-third the ratio of their population ratio to total population in the United States.

The evidence is overwhelming that the industry has brought black and other minority Americans into its numbers, at best, grudgingly. Paradoxically, the industry systematically kept minorities out of its workforce until the passage of the Civil Rights Act two decades ago. However, the industry has elected to use white women as their objects of affirmative action instead of minorities, for whom the laws were initially enacted.

In this regard, while the relative number of black Americans increased from less than ½ of 1 percent of the industry managers in 1960 to 4.3 percent in 1981, the number of white women increased from 9 percent to 32 percent as the percentage of their workforce participation. We emphasize that this is not an indictment of white women. They are not the decision makers. This is an indictment of top management of the industry, who have chosen to pit white women against minorities and in the process have frustrated the intent of the civil rights laws of the United States.

OPPORTUNITIES IN THE INDUSTRY

Black Americans believe that the banking industry does not provide them with equitable career opportunities. In fact, eight out of ten black Americans believe that white Americans enjoy greater opportunities in the industry than do minorities. As a consequence, they are ambivalent about their opportunities in the field. On a scale of one to ten, our respondents gave the industry a five with respect to whether or not they have good career prospects in it. This bland "here today and gone tomorrow" attitude augurs poorly for those responsible for managing the environment within which this potentially valuable resource functions.

THE PROBLEMS

The most significant problems, as perceived by our respondents, were (1) not knowing what is going on around them, or not being plugged into the network, (2) racism, and (3) the inability to get a mentor, in that order.

While the presence of racism resists definitive proof, and although there are other factors involved in the process, it can be rationally argued that racism is the most fundamental reason for the fact that black and other minority Americans are not "plugged into the system" and that they cannot get mentors. Of the three significant problems cited by our respondents, racism is perhaps the most pervasive and pernicious factor that adversely affects their careers. Given these problems as perceived by our respondents, it is not surprising that almost 80 percent would leave their bank if something better came along. Obviously, one could be quite happy in a current job and still wisely leave if something better came along. Frequently, this is the only way one can grow to one's potential. No doubt, this is in part the reason behind the attitude of our respondents. Nevertheless, in the context of the findings of this research, the more plausible interpretation of their desire to leave their current bank would appear to be that they are, at best, bland in their relationship with their current institution. More likely, they are dissatisfied with their lot. This type environment exerts a downward pressure on loyalty.

Finally, exerting a major impact upon the attitude of the blacks in the banking industry is the fact that they believe that their banks have reversed their position of five or more years ago of actively attracting minorities to the industry. Thus, on a scale of one to ten, the respondents gave their bank a 3.3, suggesting that almost 70 percent of them feel that their bank has abdicated its commitment to vigorous recruitment and development of minorities in the industry.

PROMOTION CRITERIA AND DYNAMICS

In a society in which growth is synonymous with survival, the ability to get promoted on one's job is perhaps the most basic success criterion, as judged by most Americans. Given this assumption, if our respondents' perceptions are correct, getting an education, working hard, and keeping one's nose clean are not likely to get one beyond first base in the pursuit of promotions.

By a wide margin our respondents believe that the most important criterion for promotion is not hard work, or education, but "who you know." In fact, 76 percent of them believe that who you know is the most important promotion criterion. Hard work was rated eighth and education rated tenth in order of importance for promotion.

Putting these criteria in perspective, our personal interviewees indicated that education is important in one's getting the job, and hard work is important in one's keeping the job, but by themselves they are insufficient to get one promoted beyond the lower levels of management in the banking industry.

As for the promotion dynamics, 70 percent of our respondents feel that even when the promotion criteria are clearly known they are not administered fairly. In fact, they feel that mediocre white employees are likely to be promoted over superior black employees.

Perhaps the most insidious promotion dynamics which black and other minority Americans still endure is that which requires one to train his supervisor, who by training, tenure, and know-how is inferior to him or her. We were surprised to find this practice alive and well in a number of banks. These perceptions and practices obviously contribute to the high turnover and the absence of loyalty among minority employees in the banking industry.

THE QUALITY OF SUPERVISION

The immediate supervisor is perhaps more responsible for employee attitudes than any other facet of the organizational structure of the banking industry, or of any industry for that matter. Specifically, our respondents were ambivalent about the quality of their supervision.

This ambivalence regarding their supervisor is a major factor in the attitude of blacks toward the industry. The factors contributing most to the negative attitudes of black Americans toward supervisors in the industry are: (1) most supervisors do not provide either career guidance or objective feedback to the employees and (2) the supervisors generally exclude minorities from their informal job-related social dynamics, which more often than not is where important information is dispensed as to what is going on in the organization. The supervisor's behavior is unquestionably the most significant contributor to the condition that keeps minorities out of the network, or prevents them from knowing what is going on.

In terms of career guidance, black employees are left to guess where they stand with respect to performance and career opportunities.

These behavior patterns on the part of supervisors have the effect of generating insecurity, obviating loyalty to the organization, and stultifying growth of minorities in the industry. One could plausibly argue that, given an orchestrated racist environment, these behavior patterns and their results are no accident, but rather are purposely planned. In this scenario, no rational recommendation based upon sound organizational behavior will change anything. Such behavior can only be affected by economic sanctions imposed by regulatory authorities, which, incidentally, are already provided for by existing law. Evidence is overwhelming that currently the laws are being only tepidly administered by the appropriate regulatory agencies.

Despite the fact that the supervisors are less than ideal as viewed by our respondents, there is evidence which suggests that one can be successful in the corporate environment, even under hostile conditions. The behavior patterns of the employee which lead to success/ survival even under hostile supervisors supercede race and are in our opinion worthy of serious consideration by not only black and other minority Americans but by any young person seeking to build a career in the industry. (See Chapter 3 for detail.)

PEER RELATIONSHIPS

Next to the importance of the immediate supervisor with respect to career development is the nature of the relationship between an employee and his peers on the job. For best results, an employee should enjoy an easy interaction between himself and his peers. In the absence of this interaction, an employee may be left out of the communication system, which is critically important to his knowing what is going on around him.

With notable exceptions, black Americans are not plugged into their peer networks. On the contrary, not only are they systematically excluded from normal peer interaction; when they are included, the conversation frequently is likely to be superficial rather than containing the substantive information that is so common and important among peers.

When the lack of interaction with one's peers is coupled with the exclusion from social settings with one's supervisor, there is little wonder that black and other minority Americans "do not know what is going on in the organization." Clearly, this places a severe handicap on minority employees in their efforts to become aware of upcoming opportunities for advancement before they are preempted by others. In addition, it deprives them of certain fundamental informal information, about one's supervisor in particular, and about the organization in general, that may be important in one's effort to understand the difference between the formal communication system in the organization and "what really matters." This may mean the difference between one's ability to do a "mediocre" job and a "superior" job, and consequently, the difference between promotion and stagnation.

MENTORS

Unofficial in structure and in a class by themselves, mentors are as important, and in certain respects more important than supervisors, to anyone seeking to climb the corporate ladder. Mentors, having only in recent years emerged as a publicly discussed phenomenon, are those persons who are in position to assist one in the development of one's career. Typically an inconspicuous relationship, the mentor may provide the mentee career counselling and job leads within the organization before they become widely known, "run interference" for the mentee when problems beyond his control adversely affect him, and provide visibility to the mentee at appropriate times when his career may be enhanced.

The mentor-mentee relationship is like any other human relationship. One gets out of it what one puts into it. Like any human relationship, there generally is a quid pro quo. While the mentee typically is the greatest *direct* beneficiary, a *wise* mentee will always be on the lookout for opportunities to do something on behalf of the mentor. This may be no more than keeping the mentor apprised of how well the mentee has followed the advice the mentor has given and, as a result, how well he has done. For example, a mentor may have a selfish interest on behalf of his personal empire within the organization, for which the mentee may be being groomed. Or, the mentor may have the larger organization at heart, thus developing future management. It is equally plausible that the mentor may wish to see a young manager develop to his maximum potential, the reward for which, not unlike that of a teacher, is the success of the young person.

Mentors typically are not easy to get, unless one is fortunate to work for an organization that has a formally managed mentor-mentee system. Like any highly desirable commodity, mentors are in demand, and there generally are not enough of them to go around. This stems from the pyramid shape of the normal business organization. That is, the largest number of employees are at the bottom, decreasing in number as they go up the ladder, with only one at the very peak. Since there are fewer people at the top, and it is from this level that mentors are generally found, it follows that there are not likely to be enough mentors for all the young managers in the typical organization.

Thus, those employees who are successful in securing a viable mentor-mentee relationship may be considered fortunate. Given this circumstance, it stands to reason that the time of the mentor is likely to be at a premium. *The wise mentee*, therefore, *will be creative in pursuit of a mentor, judicious in the use of the mentor's time, and deft in the development and maintenance of the relationship*.

With notable exceptions, the initiative is likely to rest with the prospective mentee, that is, the mentee must find creative ways to *attract* the attention of the mentor within the context of the normal business or social setting which may prevail at a given time.

As evidenced by our respondents, black Americans, in general, do not have mentors in the banking industry. Instead, they are left to fend for themselves in an environment in which they begin as outsiders. If anyone needs mentors, it is black and other minority Americans. In fact, the inability to get a mentor was considered a very close third of the three (closely bunched) most important problems experienced by our respondents.

Our research revealed that only a few of our respondents had mentors, with women mentees outnumbering men. We should emphasize that females may encounter serious difficulties in their effort to cultivate a relationship with a male mentor. Unless carefully handled on the part of both parties, the relationship could be misunderstood and thereby cause career difficulties for either, or both. The most public example is the relationship between William Agee and Mary Cunningham, formerly president and vice-president of Bendix Corporation.

Mentors are obviously very desirable, and it is widely believed that without a mentor one is not likely to advance to upper or top management. Our research, nevertheless, reveals that those who have in fact made it to top management with the help of mentors say they could have made it without them. Obviously, while this may be true, this assertion cannot be verified.

FINANCIAL REWARDS

It is widely believed that the banking industry as a general rule does not pay salaries comparable to industry. Historically, this has been true. This is less the case today, however, than in earlier years, especially in regional and money center banks, where minorities are most likely to work. However, our respondents ranked salary as fifth in order of importance where satisfaction is concerned. Incidentally this finding agrees with satisfaction indexes of prior research of professional employees in industry, in general. At any rate, while there were exceptions, our research revealed that black Americans in general are paid commensurate with their counterparts throughout the industry for similar work. This was especially true for those with MBAs. The exceptions to this generalization tended to fall disproportionately on black women. In this regard, black men tended to earn higher salaries than black women. This was due to two major causes: (1) a carryover of the era in which women in general, and black women in particular, were not given higher paying job functions (the sexism phenomenon) and (2) black women in the banking industry on average have a lower educational level than black men. For example, our research revealed that black men held four times as many MBA degrees as black women in the banking industry. However, even with similar education levels and tenure, black men tend to earn more than black women, a practice which probably pervades the entire banking labor force without regard to race.

While our field interviews revealed that our respondents generally were paid comparably to their white peers for the same type job, they perceived, nevertheless, that the salaries for black bankers, especially males, were effectively capped by arbitrary job ceilings. A view widely held by our respondents is that black Americans are relegated to arbitrary job ceilings in the banking industry. In this regard, when black men begin to "churn" excessively at a given level, they generally choose to leave the bank. Black women, on the other hand, tend to stay and adjust to that perceived ceiling. This clearly is a contributory factor to the diminution of black men in the banking industry in comparison to black women.

THE INDUSTRY SELECTS OUT BLACK MEN

At the beginning of the 16-year period ending in 1981, black men and women were represented in about equal numbers at the management level in the banking industry. Both black males and black females increased in number slowly in the industry following the Civil Rights Act of 1964. Around 1975, the growth in numbers of black women at the management level began to accelerate in the industry, while the number of black men leveled off and have largely remained at the 1975 level as a percentage of the industry management workforce. This emerging behavior in the industry raised some serious questions in our minds, both as scholars and as black Americans. It was also one of the phenomena that we did not anticipate at the outset of our research.

In an industry that has been managed largely by men until the passage of the Civil Rights Act of 1964, it must be asked why black men are not being selected and developed into the management hierarchy of the banking industry, at a minimum, at the same level as black women?

To answer this question, we cross tabulated education and salary by sex, discovering that black men in the industry were more highly educated than black women. Black women, however, had longer tenure. It should be pointed out that tenure is a *result* and not a *cause*, with respect to this phenomenon. The evidence is convincing that black women have greater tenure because they tend to stay with the bank despite the lack of growth available to them. Black men, on the other hand, are more likely to become dissatisfied and leave the industry. Thus, while there are other important employment selection criteria, education is the only objective variable in our data that may be a selection causation agent. If the banking industry is using education as the most important selection criterion, our data indicate that black males should outnumber black females in the industry.

Since the converse of this result is, in fact, the case, we asked our personal interviewees "what dynamic was prevalent in the industry that would cause black women to be selected and retained in the banking industry in greater numbers than black men?" The response was emphatic and widespread among both black men and black women that *"Black men are systematically given a more difficult time in the industry, frequently provoking them to resign or to be fired."* In addition, black males who have the same high self-image characteristic and aggressive personality as white males must either "walk softly" or face the prospect of being driven out of the industry, out of frustration. While these latter characteristics are rewarded in white males, they appear to be a cause for punishment for black males. Black males are perceived "as more of a threat to white male supervisors than black females."

There is also the "two-for" phenomenon, which Eleanor Holmes, formerly chairman of the Equal Employment Opportunity Commission, claims is not possible under existing regulations.[1] This phenomenon is, nevertheless, still very much alive and widely discussed among minorities in the banking industry as a basis for the industry's hiring of more black females than males. Further, the evidence suggests that whether this practice is possible under current regulations or not, it appears to be working, and to the obvious detriment of black men. The "two-for" phenomenon is the practice of double counting a black woman on E.E.O.C. reports as a woman and as a minority.

TURNING BACK THE CLOCK

Regardless of the true cause of this phenomenon, this is a serious indictment of the industry. If this practice continues unabated, within the next decade or two black men will be almost nonexistent in the management hierarchy of the banking industry. *This would be a retrogression of the position of this segment of American*

*society to the pre-1964 era in the industry, and thus would usher in
a Reconstruction Era (de ja vu).*

The suppression of black men as a resource has serious implications not only for black society but also for U.S. society, in general, a discussion of which is beyond the scope of this research project. Nonetheless, as has been true throughout history, the Hand Writes on the Wall . . . and Having Written . . . Moves On.

NOTE

1. Eleanor Holmes Norton, "Struggle for the Executive Suite — Black vs. White Women," *Black Enterprise* 11 (September 1980): p. 24.

11

MAKING IT . . . ANYHOW

The findings of this research lead inexorably to the conclusion that, with notable exceptions, the banking industry poses severe obstacles to the career development process of *black* and other *minority* Americans. Another conclusion to which minorities might be led is that banking is an industry that they should avoid.

This may be an appropriate decision. Before deciding to eschew the banking industry, however, black Americans should ask the question: Is the banking industry unique in its rampant racism and the concomitant career suppression behavior? One need only peruse the literature cited in Chapter 1 to conclude that racism and discrimination are widespread throughout American industry at this point in history. What we have done is to measure, for the first time, the intensity of the attitudes and perceptions of black Americans who function in this environment. Most of the prior research has been either purely statistical conclusions, without regard to the human aspects, or journalistic conclusions, without regard to statistical support. We have sought to combine the best of both of these approaches. In the process, we have produced some landmark results. Accordingly, black and other minority Americans could easily draw the conclusion that the banking industry should be shunned at any cost.

Such a decision, however, would be analogous to that often made by casual observers of the medical profession in situations in which it is thought that there is an increase in a given disease in the country at a given time when, in fact, the increase is a result of improved reporting and diagnostic mechanisms. In other words, the behavior we have documented is neither new nor unique to the banking industry. Our study simply measures this behavior more accurately and comprehensively than have prior studies.

Racism is deeply rooted in the American culture. Moreover, it appears to run in cycles, in consonance with the leadership of the country at a given time in history. In periods in which racism is held to be un-American and unacceptable by the top level leadership of the nation, racism takes a downward turn, or goes underground. Conversely, when racism appears to be acceptable behavior by top leaders of the nation, it emerges from underground and asserts itself in many ways and in many places.

That racism is still very much a pervasive phenomenon in American society was best articulated in an article by Hodding Carter, III, which appeared in the *Wall Street Journal* April 26, 1984:

> Thirty-five years ago, it was possible to sing the line from "South Pacific" about having to "be taught to hate and fear" and go off into the sunset believing that the answer to racism could be found in education and positive thinking. Three decades of grudging, gradual but in many ways monumental progress later, it seems a quaint notion. Every step forward, to the side and back has been marked by immense effort, bloodshed, political turmoil and *vicious* (italics supplied) resistance. In the collective national pause of the past few years, it has become clear that there is still a long way to go — which comes as a disturbing revelation to many whites, but is a basic fact of life for most minorities.[1]

The only effective way to ameliorate the practice of racism in this country, in our opinion, is to use economic sanctions that are severe enough to serve as a deterrent. Advocates notwithstanding, the evidence is overwhelming that voluntary constraints do not work in substantive ways.

If we proceed under the assumption that racism is likely to be prevalent throughout industry for an indeterminate future period, black Americans and other minority groups must address the question: "If we shun the banking industry, what is the alternative?"

While the alternative may vary in degree, with respect to racism, the evidence suggests that minorities cannot escape the problems of racism by shunning the banking industry. Moreover, since banking is the institution that provides the working capital on which the American economic system functions, it possesses the power base to determine who will grow and who will stagnate and who will build a wealth base and who will not.

As detestable as it is, given the universal fact of racism in American industry, coupled with the pivotal role of the banking industry in the American economy, logic suggests that black and other minority Americans would be abdicating their access to the most fundamental power source in our economic system if they shunned the banking industry. We believe, therefore, that it is in the long-term interest of black and other minority Americans to continue to pursue careers in the banking industry, not as meek, dependent personalities, but as creative, alert tacticians who understand the forces with which they must contend, striking a blow for change when the opportunity presents itself, but in the meantime, "strategically rolling with the punch."

UNDERSTANDING THE ENVIRONMENT

This analysis proceeds under the assumption that if minority Americans are to succeed in industry, the first step is to understand the environment of industry in general. Many behavioral dynamics of industry supercede race, and some of these practices may be misconstrued as having racial overtones when they may not. We are not suggesting that race can be ignored. We are saying that if one understands how the system works, without regard to race, it then becomes easier to isolate the purely racist behavior. This leaves more creative energy to attack the fundamental problems that would otherwise be dissipated on issues that appear racist, when they may, in fact, not be. Accordingly, in the sections which follow, we will set forth some determinants of success that may be helpful to minorities who may wish to pursue careers in the industry, racism notwithstanding.

DETERMINANTS OF SUCCESS

We believe that it is useful to divide the determinants of success in the corporate arena into two broad classes, in much the same manner as industry frequently does in evaluating managers of various functions within the corporate structure, that is, those which are within the direct control of the manager and those over which he may have varying degrees of control.

This is not meant to be an exhaustive treatment of how to succeed in the corporate world. Instead, it is designed to cover the most important issues which we believe deserve consideration, given the problems which surfaced during the course of our research.

Within this context, those factors falling within the control of the individual employee are: a comprehensive assessment of oneself, followed by a similar assessment of the specific job in which an employee finds himself. Following these assessments, there are a number of factors in the general category of *managing oneself*. Within this broad category fall the management of one's *image, career path, politics, networks,* and *stress*. The final success determinant within the control of the employee is the *evaluation of one's career* at its various stages.

Those determinants which fall within the category over which an employee has some, but not decisive, control are: *the management of one's boss* and the *acquisition of a mentor*.

We have elected to devote most of this chapter to those factors within the control of the employee for two reasons. First, we believe that they are the most important determinants of success; and second, we believe that it would be unnecessarily redundant to treat supervisory management and mentoring here since they have been adequately covered in earlier chapters.

IS THIS THE JOB FOR ME?

In the personal interview component of our research, we encountered a number of interviewees who seriously questioned whether or not they had reached, or could reach, their full potential in their current jobs. We were not surprised at this phenomenon. Since two of the target markets for this book are minorities currently employed by the banking industry who might still be trying to "find their way" and those college students, graduate and undergraduate, who may be contemplating a career in the industry, it occurred to us that a section on matching *self* and *job* may be of some value. We further thought, however, that since the majority of our readers are likely to be college students or college graduates, it would be redundant to exhaustively treat this issue here. Therefore, we decided to treat only the highlights.

SELF-ASSESSMENT

The first step in determining whether a given job is the appropriate one is to make an objective assessment of oneself. Specifically, one should take a conscious inventory (in fact, written) of one's interests, skills, both physical and mental, knowledge base, and value system. A careful and systematic analysis of these factors as they relate to one's personality cannot be overemphasized. Unless one understands oneself, one is likely to flounder aimlessly through one's working life, never quite understanding why things happen.

ASSESSING THE JOB

Having made an introspective analysis of oneself, the next step in the drive to success in the corporate arena is to make an assessment of the job. A number of factors should be considered in the analysis of the job. Among the most important are: (1) What is the objective or purpose of the job? (2) How does it fit into the total scheme of the organization? (3) What are the specific duties associated with the job? (4) What is the bottom line that must be achieved by the job assignment? (5) What kind of time pressures are associated with the job? (6) What specific skills or knowledge base is required? (7) To what degree does success in the job depend upon others, both within the department, and elsewhere? (8) Where does this job lead?

ASSESSING THE CLIMATE

These job factors are self-evident and do not require elaboration. Perhaps the most important one in the analysis of the job is the climate within which one functions. Assessment of the climate is much more complex and deserves careful analysis on the part of the employee if he expects to succeed. *It is the organizational climate that determines the ease or difficulty with which the job can be accomplished.*

There are a number of approaches to analysis of the climate of an organization. One such approach we think is comprehensive is the House and Rizzo Organizational Practice Questionnaire. This questionnaire, comprising 14 questions, covers such management issues as the decision-making process, the reporting requirements of the job, the information flow process, up, down, and horizontal, job descriptions, performance and promotion standards, teamwork, and intergroup cooperation[2] (see Table 11.1).

A perusal of the questions in this questionnaire suggests that this is not an exercise that can be superficially executed. Instead, it requires careful and systematic research, deft inquiry among peers, and careful observation. The questionnaire cannot be completed at one interview session, or with one or two people. Instead, it must be pursued systematically and methodically over an indeterminate time frame, sometimes unobtrusively, at other times, directly, with any number of persons in or outside the organization. The responses to the questionnaire should be written and upon completion carefully studied for patterns of behavior that may characterize the climate of the firm.

Once the climate of the organization becomes clear, one can then gauge one's chances of success within that structure; and in the process, one may plan strategy for survival either in an inhospitable climate or success in a positive climate, whichever the case may be.

MANAGING ONESELF

If one took an objective look back over one's past, no doubt one would discern that most of the problems stemmed from one's own behavior rather than from someone else's. This gives credence to the adage that "we are our own worst enemy." This is not a black or white connotation. It is a human characteristic. If one accepts this assumption, it would seem to follow that *most* of the rational factors affecting one's career fall under one's personal responsibility. Since racism is an irrational phenomenon, it falls into the exception category. As difficult as it is, however, a significant number of minorities manage to negotiate around racism in their career pursuit. We emphasize, however, that we have no magic formula for the solution to racism, although we have some ideas

TABLE 11.1
House and Rizzo Organizational Climate Dimensions

---

1. Timely decision making: Are consistent guidelines for work communicated?
2. Upward informational requirements: How much detailed technical and administrative information is required by superiors in the organization?
3. Top management receptiveness: How much interest in and evaluation do top managers give to ideas from subordinates?
4. Induction and/or promotion of those outside the organization: How much does management fill positions from within and from outside the organization?
5. Formalization: Are job descriptions, performance standards, and appraisals established in writing and readily available?
6. Selection criteria based on ability: Are promotions based on performance or "playing politics"?
7. Job pressure: How much work is assigned and how much time is required to complete it?
8. Subordinate development: What are the expectations of top management regarding subordinate instruction and career development, and what are the rewards given for carrying out these expectations?
9. Teamwork: How does one's work group work together and accept changes?
10. Intergroup cooperation: Is there cooperation among work groups in the performance of work?
11. Chain of command: What is the degree to which direct orders come only from immediate supervisors?
12. Information distortion and suppression: To what degree is necessary information distorted?
13. General communication: What is the general state of communication in the organization?
14. Definition of work: To what degree is the job defined?

Source: Joseph Raelin, *The Salaried Professional — How to Make the Most of Your Career* (New York: Praeger, 1984), pp. 171-72.

that may be of modest value. This section on managing oneself, in our view, includes the most important set of factors which determine the success or failure of those who seek careers in the corporate arena.

MANAGING ONE'S IMAGE

One of the most important criteria for success is the image one projects of oneself, or how one is perceived within the organization. Research by Clubert and McDonugh concluded that if one is to succeed in the business arena, one must establish a set of images that will cause one's contributions first to be recognized and then to be valued.[3]

Do you know what your image is in your church? . . . in your social or business organization? . . . among your peers? . . . your subordinates? . . . or among your superiors? Should you be concerned about it? Is it important?

The answer to the last two questions is *yes*. One's image is very important in the development of a career and one should be constantly concerned about it. While one's image is the perception of others regarding oneself, it is the person's responsibility to shape that image. *We emphasize here that we do not suggest that one should devote useful time to the artificial or superficial machinations of image building.* This will be recognized early in the game for what it is: *meaningless, self-serving posturing.* Should such an image develop among one's associates and superiors, one is essentially dead, in terms of growth in that organization, and justly so.

What we refer to here is the systematic but subtle approach to making sure that the good work which one plans or is currently doing is seen in its proper perspective by those directly and indirectly concerned with that work.

TAKING ON DIFFICULT TASKS

One of the most effective ways to build a good reputation is to take on high risk tasks and give them everything one has. For example, in describing why Citicorp has emerged as the world's largest and most efficiently managed bank, *Business Week* stated:

> Citicorp's heroes are workers who have undertaken formidable tasks and scored big victories. . . . ask about risk-takers, and Citi insiders will mention Vice Chairman John Reed with reverence. Reed is a legend because he persevered through the dark years of 1980 and 1981, when the now-successful individual bank was filling up the huge losses that earned him the wrath of both Wall Street and managers in other parts of the bank, who were angry about losing their business because Reed red ink was erasing Citi's profits. . . . [Reed was named Chairman of Citicorp at the age of 45 shortly after this article was published] .[4]

Obviously, only a few Americans can aspire to the chairmanship of the world's largest bank. The principle here is not Citicorp, or John Reed, but building careers through risk at every level of career development, from trainee status to the chairmanship.

Accordingly, those who seek to move above the crowd would be wise to be on the lookout for such opportunities. In other words, it may be well to remember that problems are opportunities turned inside out.

For example, if one is given a task that carries with it high risk, but which also could be highly visible, an effective approach to image management would be to state in writing what one hopes to achieve, including a delineation of the risks and the likelihood of success or failure. This memorandum should be circulated to those both directly and indirectly affected. This has the effect of enhancing one's image, no matter which way the event falls. Plunging into high risk tasks and succeeding or failing without first setting the stage for possible outcome and appropriate communication follow-up is working hard, but not working smart. And, as our respondents revealed, hard work by itself is not likely to get one very far up the corporate ladder.

Finally, having completed the task, if the results are not positive, one has already set the stage initially for this possibility. If they are favorable, however, a follow-up memorandum should be sent to appropriate persons in the organization setting forth the positive result. Under either condition, care should be taken to give as much credit as possible to those persons without whose assistance one could not have achieved that result. What one has succeeded in doing is making selected people in the organization feel good because they have been given credit (and this should be genuine), while at the same time one has established an image of getting difficult tasks done.

Obviously, if the results are negative, the memorandum should report all the effort that went into the project, including the assistance of those who, in fact, did help, with one taking care to reference the original memorandum. No one should expect accolades for failure. Nonetheless, to minimize the negative impact of failure on one's image, one must position oneself up front in a manner that will neutralize the impact of the failure.

One's total image is composed of a combination of factors, each contributing to the totality in accordance with its import. In addition to the quality of one's work, one's dress, speech, habits, self-control, behavior under pressure, and ability to work as a team member are equally important in the shaping of one's image.

MANAGING ONE'S APPEARANCE

Total appearance cannot be overestimated. This is the first image criterion that others are able to see and from which they make judgments. The first impression is difficult to shake, whether it is good or bad. In this regard, every institution has a dress code. Some firms, I.B.M. for example, articulate theirs. (See the white shirt/blouse and gray or blue pinstripe.) Others do not articulate theirs. But the code is equally as significant, whether it is explicit or implicit. Persons who do not observe the dress code are likely to find themselves left out of what is going on around them and are likely to see their careers stunted.

Equally important in the development of one's image is one's communication skills, both oral and written. The ability to use Standard English and to speak easily is one of the highest success criteria, as evidenced by our survey respondents as well as other research results. For many black Americans, this entails a significant change in their speech habits. The kind of speech that is popular in many black communities, especially among the youth, will not contribute to success in the corporate arena. If one cannot use Standard English in an easy flow, one is likely to be passed over for assignments which involve public contact. Similarly, the ability to write concisely, correctly, and persuasively is equally important. As a manager, loan officer, or other staff officer, one will be called upon frequently to prepare written analyses of problems and to recommend solutions for busy superiors. Regardless of the quality of its substance, a report prepared with poor syntax that is verbose and lacking in coherence is likely to elicit negative responses. In the process, such reports exert a negative impact on one's image.

Self-control is another important image criterion. Persons unable to control their emotions, even in difficult situations, are likely to be labelled unstable and unable to take the pressure that is often associated with banking or other corporate business.

BEING A TEAM PLAYER

Finally, being perceived as a team member is critically important to anyone's success in the corporate world. Such factors as getting along with one's peers, being flexible in work assignments when the need arises, and offering to assist others in case of emergencies are among the behavior patterns that go into shaping a team member's image in the organization. We emphasize here that our personal interviews revealed that one cannot expect to be promoted to a position of importance unless there is absolutely no doubt in the minds of those making the decision that the employee "can be trusted" and "is a team player."

From the above, it is clear that one's image emerges from a combination of behavior patterns, each at the initiative of the employee. While care must be taken not to leave one's image to chance, in the final analysis, it must result from the kind of person one naturally projects oneself to be, that is, the quality of one's work and how one relates to others. Whatever image emerges in the environment within which one works will determine the growth potential of that employee.

MANAGING ONE'S CAREER PATH

Career paths naturally evolve from three basic functions: one's understanding of oneself, one's understanding of the job from which the path will emanate, and finally, one's understanding of the organizational environment within which the career path must develop. While the concept of a career path is not complex in and of itself, dependent upon the attitudes and practices of management, career paths can run the gamut from a subjective feeling about a series of jobs over an unspecified time frame to an objective description which can lead in many directions — upward, downward, diagonally, or horizontally.[5]

If one is fortunate over the life of one's career, one will have satisfied what Maslow described as all five stages of human needs: (1) physiological, (2) safety, (3) social, (4) self-esteem, and (5) self-actualization.[6] The physiological stage speaks to the need for food, clothing, shelter, medical care, etc., or one's basic survival needs. The safety level relates to the need for tenure on the job, pension plans, insurance programs, savings, etc. The social needs represent one's need to belong in one's organization and to be accepted in social interaction among one's work associates. The fourth level, self-esteem, represents the need for responsibility, achievement, challenge, and recognition. The final need, self-actualization, represents a level which few in society achieve, total self-acceptance resulting from achievement of one's full potential.[7]

Reflection upon the above career needs hierarchy permits one to easily conclude that in the early stages one is likely to devote most of one's time to the achievement of the first two stages, although the fortunate ones may also achieve varying degrees of three and four.

As one moves up the career ladder, those needs that have already been met become less important. This gives credence to the fact that our respondents rated salary level fifth on their hierarchy of job satisfaction. After the basic needs of an employee have been met, logically those needs at the higher ends of the job satisfaction hierarchy take on increased importance.

Armed with an understanding of the needs one strives to satisfy during the evolution of a career, one can begin to conceptualize a possible "career anchor." The career anchor evolves from one's talent, abilities, motives, needs, attitudes, and values as perceived by oneself. According to Edgar Stein's research, career anchors typically are not stable or rigid in the formative years, but rather evolve with experience. But once formed, they remain relatively stable throughout one's career.[8]

One's career can evolve around two major anchors and six supporting ones. The two major anchors are: (1) technical/functional and (2) managerial. The supporting anchors are: (1) security, (2) autonomy, (3) creativity, (4) service, (5) identity, and (6) variety.[9]

Whether or not one achieves one's career objectives is a function of a number of factors, the most important of which is management's attitude toward career development. Equally important are introspection and the planning of and vigor with which one pursues career goals. Of the above factors, the most important is the latter. In the final analysis, one's success is a function of one's own efforts. Even with a management planned and directed career development program, the primary responsibility for career development rests with the employee. Aside from the help one may get from a mentor, professionals cannot expect that their management is going to plan their career for them.[10]

This conclusion becomes even more critical to black and other minority Americans whose career pursuits are often thwarted by a lack of information flow in their direction, as our research demonstrated. Minorities, therefore, would be wise not to expect to receive substantive career assistance from their supervisors. Instead, they should be exceptionally creative in their search for information regarding careers. The creative interaction with peers and others who may have relevant information regarding career alternatives in one's organization, supplemented by careful observation and mentor assistance (if available) may be the most effective alternative to effective career planning and pursuit for minority employees.

The anchors set forth above are self-explanatory and need little or no elaboration here. Students of management will quickly interpret the two basic anchors as the classical structures of all organizations: line and staff functions. Line functions involve the decision makers or those responsible for the bottom line. Staff functions, on the other hand, involve those with technical expertise who give advice or make recommendations to the line officers. Neither function should be viewed as good or bad, per se. Instead, these career anchors should be seen as flowing from one's personality and interest. One need not preclude the other. A person may move easily from one to the other and be equally productive. In fact, the needs of the organization determine where minorities may be placed. Since employees in staff functions do not give orders, the perception of some white managers that minorities can be tolerated more easily in these positions leads them to persuade minorities to accept them, or to assign minorities disproportionately to staff responsibilities.

With respect to the six supporting anchors, it is easy to see that the weight one places on these factors is a function of personality. A person, for example, who emphasizes security, is likely to place less weight on autonomy and identity. Conversely, a person who places a premium on identity and autonomy is likely to put less weight on security. One can be creative, seek variety and want to render service regardless of the other anchors.

MANAGING ONE'S POLITICS

Perhaps the most important determinant of whether or not career goals are achieved may be how well one understands the politics of the organization and how well one manages one's personal politics.

Although all forms of organizational analysis are important in career development, even in the most cordial climate one will be unable to achieve career fulfillment if one neglects to observe the appropriate political tactics prevalent in the organization. It is critical that one "fit in" if one is to achieve the optimal mutual acceptance with one's colleagues. Politics is both a way of speeding up and ensuring that one attains the third stage of human needs in work settings, that of mutual acceptance.[11]

It may be recalled that our respondents overwhelmingly selected "who you know" or "politics" as the most important criterion for getting ahead in the organization. Even so, most employees in work settings use the word "politics" derisively. The term typically conjures up visions of evil people without merit scheming and plotting to get ahead, at the expense of more deserving employees. In the real world, there is some truth in that point of view. On the other hand, realistically one must realize that politics enters even the most basic organization of our society, the family. Politics therefore pervades all organizational behavior, whether the organization is large or small, profit or nonprofit, private or public.

Since politics does, in fact, play a critical part in organizational life, it might be useful for the astute employee to view it in another light. Weiler believes that politics does not have to connote unethical compromise or manipulation. He prefers to define it as: "An astute awareness of human dimensions . . . and . . . a carefully, consciously

developed set of interpersonal competencies [for using that aware-
ness] to accomplish change or improvement."[12] Thus, while politics
uses influence and power for one's selfish ends, it need not necessarily connote sinister behavior, or be practiced at unfair expense
to others. In this regard, since most organizations have a formalized
set of rules, regulations, standards, and controls by which they are
administered, generally an informal pattern of behavior will emerge
as a means of getting things done. This informal behavior may not
be in defiance of the formal rules (although this happens), but rather
simplifies and shortcuts the formal process. Politics, in this setting,
is no more than learning how this informal process functions and
plugging into it.

Clearly, politics is more complex than the above scenario. There
obviously are circumstances in which it is used deviously by people
without merit as a means of getting things done. To suggest that
this does not happen would be tantamount to suggesting that we do
not have crime in the United States, or that it is always sought out
and punished. Neither of the above scenarios is true, nor is there an
absence of devious politics in corporate America. Just as citizens
must be aware of (not necessarily tolerate) an imperfect society,
corporate employees must be aware of imperfect corporate behavior.
Under these conditions, white Americans along with black Americans
suffer alike, albeit clearly black and other minority Americans
suffer more.

While there are no "fail-safe" guidelines for determining specific
political strategies for an individual in corporate organizations,
Raelin suggests five tactics that may be of help to one in the management of politics in the world of business. They are:

1. Managing Organizational Symbolism — Here, one needs to keenly
    discern, understand, and meticulously observe the symbols used
    in the organization to get things done: such symbols as speech,
    dress, mannerisms, and most importantly, "how things are done
    around here." Reckless disregard of any one of these symbols
    may relegate the employee to the sidelines.
2. Managing a Good Image — Every organization has an image that
    is unique to that organization. Understanding what the image is
    and striving to emulate and contribute to it is a must if one is
    to be an insider in an organization. (One's personal image was
    treated in a prior section and requires no further treatment here.)

3. Managing Information — Perhaps the most important source in the development of one's career is relevant information. Three types of information are considered useful in this context. The first is work related, that is, technical know-how, systems, controls, etc. The second is inside information regarding the talents and weaknesses of fellow employees, superiors, and subordinates. The third class, and perhaps the most elusive, is information as to "how things really work around here."

   As our research revealed, a perception is that information is being withheld from black Americans. It should be emphasized here that while blacks may be the most deprived of relevant information, they are not alone in this deprivation. Since information is such a valued commodity, it is predictable that it is likely to be guarded zealously.

   Successful acquisition of information is a function of building trusting relationships among peers and others, typically on a mutuality of interest basis. This obviously takes time. But time in and of itself will not accomplish this result. It has to be worked at continuously and systematically. Once one is perceived as a storehouse of relevant information, it is possible to build a mutual base of political support in the organization.

4. Plugging into Decision Making — Typically, decision making is not a unilateral function in most corporations. Most decisions are a function of information gathering and analysis, report writing and recommendation, and finally the decision. To the extent that an employee can be a part of the decision-making process, personal credibility in the organization is enhanced. Care should be exercised to ascertain where others are who will be affected by the decision. This will determine how one should position oneself, either publicly or subdued. Once one is seen as associated with good decisions, it is possible to build a base of political support among peers, subordinates, and superiors.

5. Managing the Support Base — As set forth above, one's political base may be composed of a combination of subordinates, peers, and superiors. One approach to solidifying one's image of being on the right side of decisions is to astutely feel out decision participants prior to official meetings. Critical decisions frequently are made before the official meeting. An understanding of the direction of the decision before the meeting facilitates the image of being on the winning side of decisions. Being on

the right side of decisions can facilitate an image of being able to "get things done." Subordinates and peers, as well as superiors, will view one in a positive light if one is seen as having good judgment and the ability to get things done.

6. Finally, Getting to Know the Right People — As our respondents revealed, getting ahead is influenced heavily by "who you know." Proceeding under this assumption, one cannot leave to chance this important step in managing the politics. In fact, the wise employee will be on the lookout constantly for the "movers and shakers" both within and outside the organization. Developing a relationship with one or more of these persons must be carefully orchestrated. Contacts must be made as a result of natural business interest, which might take the form of seeking advice or the opinion of an expert on a matter on which one is working. Superficial approaches will be seen as self-serving and a waste of the time of the person whose interest is being sought. To the extent that one has opportunities to use social settings for these contacts, the approach is easier and often more productive. For this reason, it is very important for an employee who wishes to be "in the know" to take every opportunity to attend social functions where "movers and shakers" may be in attendance. Being perceived by peers and subordinates as one who interacts easily with persons of perceived power, whether as mentors or not, will cast the employee in a favorable political light.[13]

MANAGING ONE'S NETWORK

Networking in recent years has become a much talked about phenomenon. It is a relationship that is perceived as mutually beneficial to members. Networks can be a source of important information about what is going on in the organization, about people, those to cultivate and those to avoid, about systems or technology, about problems and solutions, and about goals and strategies. The members of networks may be peers, subordinates, friends and acquaintances within or outside the organization. Networks may be fostered by formal organization or by individuals. In the final analysis, it is the responsibility of the individual to initiate relationships leading to networking. To take a "laid back" approach to networking is to be left on the sidelines.

Networks are vitally important in the successful pursuit of a career. Like every human relationship, there must be a continuous mutuality of interest and a spirit of mutual trust. Without these two characteristics, no network relationship will endure. Properly managed, networks can be vital adjuncts in one's efforts to climb the corporate ladder.

Our research revealed that some banking institutions tend to look with disdain upon the efforts of black Americans to network within the bank during business hours. Some even go so far as to warn black employees against such relationships. The irony of this behavior on the part of white employees in the banking industry is that, on the one hand, they often thwart black employees' attempts to associate with them on an informal basis, yet they look with disfavor upon black employees who attempt to form their own network. Moreover, networking during business hours among white employees is taken for granted and is continuously practiced.

This is an unfortunate attitude on the part of white employees and deserves the attention of top management. However, until such time as top management initiates efforts to ameliorate this problem, it may be wise for black and other minority employees to network on their own time. We found that many are already pursuing this approach. While this strategy is a bit less convenient, it can be as effective as networking during office hours.

MANAGING STRESS

Stress is a part of many of life's endeavors. It certainly is a part of most work situations. To manage stress properly, one must first understand its nature, its fundamental causes, how to avoid it when appropriate, how to live with it when it cannot be avoided, and how to neutralize it when it is excessive.

All stress is not bad. Stress that motivates one to do one's best or to risk failure at a given endeavor, or that motivates one to expend energy in self-improvement in order to maintain one's job or to move up the job ladder is a positive force in one's life. Stress, like pain, may be a warning that something is wrong and that something must be done to ameliorate the problem.

In this discussion, we are limiting our scope to the stress associated with work, although it may manifest itself in many aspects of life. Stress associated with one's job typically stems from a number of sources. Among the most important are the nature of the relationship with one's boss, peers, customers, and subordinates.

Stress associated with one's boss generally results from ambiguity of assignment, excessive workload, lack of feedback regarding the quality of one's work, lack of career guidance, and of information from the boss regarding what is going on in the organization generally and, in general, the management style employed by the boss. With respect to black Americans, in addition to the above, stress may stem from overt and covert racism. Obviously, racism and other sources of job stress are not mutually exclusive phenomena. Where racism exists, it may pervade any of the other sources of job stress.

Stress associated with peers may result from their efforts to exclude one from their informal social interaction, where often information vital to one's career is discussed. It may result from the subtle efforts of peers to either make one look bad in a given work situation as a means of gaining an advantage or their refusal to cooperate where the job requires it.

Stress associated with subordinates may stem from their covert lack of cooperation, their questioning of one's knowledge as a supervisor, or their making "end runs" around one to higher levels of authority. Stress can also stem from bank customers who make end runs around the black banker.

As an example, a number of our respondents who were loan calling officers reported situations in which their customers implicitly questioned their knowledge or their ability to speak for the bank. We uncovered situations in which young bankers who were assistant vice-presidents or below were assigned to a market in which the customer base was composed of senior executives of major corporations. Such relationships typically are handled by senior bank executives of comparable stature to the client executive. Senior executives of major firms feel their time is wasted when the relationship officer is below their stature or cannot speak with confidence about what the bank can do in their behalf. In addition, the client may feel that the bank does not hold the relationship in high regard when they send an inexperienced junior officer to handle the relationship.

While frustrations of new call officers are common in situations like this, even when the bank fully supports them, our respondents felt they were being programmed to fail. They indicated that neither young black nor young white bankers can effectively handle a relationship with a major corporation unless the bank supports them in the same manner as if they were senior bank officers. Even when there is complete bank support for the young officer, the customer may feel the bank is condescending to his firm.

Having identified the most significant sources of job stress, we now turn to the management of stress. As the first step, one should seek to understand the motivation for the behavior of the person(s) who constitutes the source of the stress. It is conceivable that the behavior is unthinking and inadvertent. This is where superior interpersonal and political skills are important. These skills are needed in answering such questions as: What are the strengths and weaknesses of the person at issue? What are his alliances in the organization? If I confront him, what are his possible responses and what do I do in the event of either alternative response? Once the answers to the above questions are analyzed, an effective course of action will usually become evident.

It is rarely wise to approach a fellow employee in a confrontational manner, whether that person is the boss, a peer, or a subordinate. A pleasant nonaccusing voice is usually the best initial strategy. If, in fact, the person is guilty of what one suspects, this approach allows the person a face-saving option. If he is innocent, one has avoided a false accusation.

It is also rarely wise to sit back and expect the source of the stress to go away of its own volition. Although there are risks associated with one's efforts to solve problems, there are also risks associated with ignoring problems, thinking that they will just go away. The solution thus lies in judging the risk trade-offs. We emphasize here that, as in the case of life in general, one should not expect positive change unless one is willing to take some risks. The secret is to heed the stress warning, and then after careful evaluation of the situation, to do something.

There are no pat prescriptions that one can follow in situations such as these. Hanging on the walls of many executives is a short prayer by an anonymous author that may be worth considering. It reads: "God, grant me the serenity to accept the things I cannot change, the courage to change the things I can, and wisdom to know the difference."

One might add that wisdom comes only with experience. We are not born with it, and it cannot be taught. In cases in which one has to live with the sources of stress, a number of activities will help. Contemporary literature is flooded with books and articles on stress management. Given the stress we encountered among our interviewees, we encourage our readers to avail themselves of one or more books that treat this subject comprehensively.

In the meantime, one can engage in a number of activities, including regular physical exercise, developing a hobby, engaging in creative expression outside the workplace, getting involved in civic activity, and as a last resort, seeking alternative employment.

We emphasize that unless one finds creative release from job-related stress, one frequently begins to behave erratically, often irrationally, to the detriment of both health and work. A vicious cycle sets in. The employee is reacting to the stress caused by problems created by someone else and is subsequently judged negatively by his superiors (and, frequently, his subordinates and his peers) because as a result of these problems he cannot work efficiently. We encountered a number of instances of interviewees who themselves either had experienced this situation, or were aware of colleagues who had. In addition, we were made aware of local National Association of Urban Bankers (NAUB) chapters sponsoring stress management seminars. One such chapter made both video and cassette tapes for distribution for follow-up purposes.

SUCCESS DETERMINANTS OUTSIDE
THE CONTROL OF THE EMPLOYEE

As stated in the introduction of this chapter, we feel that it would be redundant to treat the management of one's boss and mentoring in this section, although we believe these factors to be very important. Accordingly, the reader is referred to Chapters 3 and 5 respectively for a discussion of these success determinants. We emphasize, however, that although the management of one's boss or mentor is not totally within one's control, the quality and success of these relationships rest, in large measure, on the creativity, imagination, and interpersonal skills which the employee brings to them.

CAREER EVALUATION

No matter how well a plan of any sort is executed, the result can be no better than the plan itself. The only way to ascertain the quality of the plan, as well as the execution process, is to conduct a systematic follow-up evaluation. This is no less true with respect to one's career path. Accordingly, in this section we will cover briefly the steps in the evaluation process of one's career path. The evaluation process can be divided into three steps: assessment, feedback, and reassessment.[14]

The assessment stage involves an objective self-examination of one's progress toward the goals one established for oneself. The concept of a career path connotes movement. Thus as change takes place, settings change. One therefore would be wise to write down the milestones one set for oneself at the planning stage of one's career evolution. To have accomplished those milestones would obviously be considered a success. On the other hand, one need not have failed just because one did not reach those milestones. There may have been extenuating circumstances or it may be clear from hindsight that the milestones were not realistic to begin with. Of course, one can fall into the trap of rationalizing failures; that is, one may be less than objective about oneself.

It is for this reason that one moves to the feedback stage of the evaluation process. This stage consists of eliciting objective feedback from trusted persons in position to have observed one's career behavior. One would be wise to avoid including in the feedback group persons who cannot be objective because of personal relationships. For best results, those providing feedback must feel free to be totally candid in both the positive and the negative aspects of the evaluation. Otherwise, the counsel is meaningless.

This obviously is a private affair and should be treated in that manner. Ideally, one's boss and one's mentor (assuming there is one) should be among those from whom one seeks advice.

Having obtained the feedback from others, one is then in position to contrast or compare the opinions of others with one's own assessment. Where there are differences, further assessment may be required. Where there are exceptions, the opinion of others is likely to be closer to reality. They, therefore, should be given careful consideration.

This, then, leads one to the reassessment stage. How should one restructure a career path? Should the goals be scaled down, raised, changed altogether, or should they remain the same? Thoughtful reflection on the environmental forces affecting the career to date, the opinions of others, and an objective evaluation of one's personal aspirations should enable an employee to redefine his career path with more realistic and achievable goals. The career path management process then begins anew with a more realistic view of one's career potential and more appropriate strategy for achieving that potential.

NOTES

1. Hodding Carter, III, "The U.S. Has Yet to Expunge the Stain of Racism," *Wall Street Journal* 26 (April 1984): 29.

2. Joseph Raelin, *The Salaried Professional — How to Make the Most of Your Career* (New York: Praeger, 1984), pp. 171-72.

3. Samuel A. Culbert and John J. McDonugh, *The Invisible War: Pursuing Self-Interest at Work* (New York: John Wiley and Sons, 1980), p. 22.

4. "The New Shape of Banking," *Business Week*, June 18, 1984, p. 107.

5. Raelin, *The Salaried Professional*, p. 143.

6. Ibid., p. 68.

7. Ibid., p. 143.

8. Edgar H. Stein, *Career Dynamics: Matching Individual and Organizational Needs* (Reading, Mass.: Addison-Wesley, 1978), p. 125.

9. Thomas J. Delong, "Re-examining the Career Anchor Model," *Personnel* 59 (1982): 50-61.

10. Raelin, *The Salaried Professional*, p. 1.

11. Ibid., p. 1.

12. Nichols Weiler, *Reality and Career Planning* (Reading, Mass.: Addison-Wesley, 1977), p. 22.

13. Raelin, *The Salaried Professional*, pp. 193-96.

14. Ibid., p. 260.

12

TOP MANAGEMENT: ARE YOU LISTENING?

In recent years, the Japanese Industrial Machine has been the marvel not only of its U.S. counterpart, but also of the rest of the industrialized world as well. The reason for this is that Japan has outproduced the rest of the world. Perhaps, more important, it has outsold the rest of the world, the United States included.

Ironically, while the United States with its sophisticated management techniques once was the unchallenged industrial leader of the world, it currently is engaged in an intensive, microscopic analysis of the management techniques of a country that built its industrial machine upon much of what it learned from the United States. Current literature is full of studies by American scholars and businessmen seeking to decipher the Japanese management mystique.

In the course of such study much has been learned about Japanese management techniques, most of it not new, however. Many writers have rationalized the superior performance of the Japanese management system as benefitting from the culture, which ties the worker to a company with a degree of loyalty that one cannot expect in this country. This rationalization, however, overlooks the fact that the cultural behavior to which these observers refer was operational long before the Japanese assumed world leadership in industrial production.

Like any complex phenomenon, the Japanese management success is a function of many things, an analysis of which is beyond the scope of this project. There is one factor, however, which increasingly observers agree, exerts a major influence upon the management success of the Japanese system. This phenomenon is referred to by various names, the most prevalent of which in the United States is *quality circles*. Quality circles, like *Hondas*, are a Japanese export to the United States. At the risk of oversimplification, quality circles is a practice that requires the participation of the person closest to the job with persons responsible for the management of the function in the development of systems that control that function. In effect, the quality circle is a *listening post* for management to the ideas of persons at every level of the hierarchy in an effort to get the *best* ideas possible for the management of a given function.

Thus while the American industrial system is built upon the practice of a management which *tells* its employees what to do, the Japanese system thrives on a practice that requires management to ask its employees, "What is the best way?" and then sees that management listens. In the process, the Japanese generate ideas which tend to be superior to those of its competitors. The irony of the Japanese success is that, taken individually, the Japanese worker is perhaps no more sophisticated than individual workers in other industrialized countries. What appears to be the difference is the *synergism* that is set in motion when employees know that management is listening.

MANAGEMENT'S SELF-INTEREST — AN EMPIRICAL EXAMPLE

If management in the banking industry chooses to listen, we believe the case is persuasive that their enlightened self-interest will be served by the effective resolution of the problems articulated by their black managers. In this regard, any one above the age of 30 can recall the period during which American mores dictated that there had to be segregation by race in the utilization of public accommodations. Black and other minority Americans were denied the use of public accommodations, and in the process, suffered severe humiliation. This situation existed because the conventional wisdom of business leaders at that time was that their white clientele would abandon them if minorities were permitted access to those facilities in the same manner as their white counterparts. Accordingly, business leaders fought bitterly to retain the status quo with respect to public accommodations. Only two short decades follow-ing desegregation of public accommodations, one would be hard pressed to find a profit-seeking business that would want to revert to the pre-1960s practices. In fact, during the height of the struggle, it became obvious that black and other minority customers were the difference between red and black ink at the bottom line for many businesses.

The same scenario was in evidence in professional sports. Which of the sports franchises now would return to the era when the sports establishment believed that black Americans could not com-pete in major league sports or that their white athletes and their white patrons would abandon them if minorities were permitted to engage in competition on the athletic field? After all, sports is big business, and nothing should be permitted to disturb the status quo.

We believe that if management would reflect upon the lessons of the eras cited above, it would conclude that its best interest would be served through the orderly resolution of the problems uncovered by this research. In addition, resolutions of the problems would put the industry in compliance with the intent and letter of the nation's laws providing for equal job opportunities, regardless of race, sex, or religious origin.

What follows in the remainder of this chapter is a list of the most important problems which militate against high productivity on the part of black managers and which impede the orderly pursuit of their careers as articulated by the black managers and profes-sionals in the banking industry. These problems, we believe, cry out for a management that will listen. Accordingly, we have included a list of suggestions which management may wish to consider in seek-ing to resolve these problems.

WHO'S TALKING?

To begin with, who are the black managers who have articulated these problems? Are they soreheads, malcontents, or the misfits? To say there were none of these sorts in the sample would be analo-gous to concluding that there were none in the industry at large, clearly not a realistic assumption. But to characterize the majority of the bankers in this way would be analogous to kicking a person into a ditch and then blaming him for being dirty, in our view. We found both men and women who felt that they were being "kicked into the ditch," but they were in the minority. We also talked to some men and women who were satisfied with their progress and optimistic about their futures.

The fullest understanding of who articulated the problems set forth below would be gained from a review of the profile of the sample respondents. Our respondents ranged from banking officer to senior vice-president, from just under 25 years of age to over 50. They earned from $25,000 annually to above $70,000. They resided in 22 different states representing all sections of the country, and worked mostly in banks with above $1 million in assets. Finally, more than 70 percent were college graduates, 40 percent of whom were MBAs. One would be hard put to conclude, therefore, that the bankers who were the subjects of this research are not a valid cross-section of black managers and professionals in the banking industry.

Finally, the authors concede that a number of the problems cited herein are not new; neither are the suggested approaches to the solution of these problems profound. What is unique about our treatment of these problems is that for the first time in history the intensity of the feelings of black managers in the banking industry has been measured, utilizing a satisfaction index with respect to the environment within which they work. In addition, while we have utilized statistics to quantify our findings, we have gone beyond the statistics to the human aspects of these problems. Although our solutions may be less than profound, we believe that there is a persuasive case for management to *act*, if for no other reason than its own self-interest. In this regard, it is remarkable how frequently the long-term interest of U.S. business is obscured by short-term considerations. For example, too often the philosophy of U.S. business is let's maximize profits this year, the long term will take care of itself. History records, however, that in the long run, the Japanese outproduced U.S. business. Frequently, only crises can get the attention of U.S. business regarding problems that by hindsight were dramatically clear at an earlier period.

Finally, we emphasize that the ideas suggested here begin with the assumption that the discriminatory behavior extant in the banking industry is a function of "passive racism," born out of historical mores that are no longer consciously practiced. These mores, like any kinetic force, continue long after the original power source has been cut off. If this assumption is *not valid*, however, the reader could wisely stop reading at this point. The rest of the chapter would be a waste of time. If, however, the assumption is valid, the ideas which follow may be of some value in assisting management to meet what should be its objective of selecting, training, and maintaining the most productive employees it can find, be they black, white, or other.

LIMITATIONS

As set forth earlier, we consciously elected to research only one side of the issues covered in this project, that is, the perceptions of black managers as to what is happening around them and how it is affecting them. Obviously, additional research needs to be done to assess management's view of these issues. Such additional research may or may not corroborate the views of our respondents. Whether it does or not does not obviate the problems articulated by these bankers. Those skilled in sound human relations management know that the perception of problems by employees, real or imagined, must be addressed with equal commitment in either case, lest they fester and get worse. It seems to us, therefore, that the *increasingly competitive, highly people oriented business* suggests that *people, not money*, is the industry's most important asset. To dissipate a significant share of this asset, as the industry appears to be doing, defies rational management from any perspective.

TOP MANAGEMENT'S ROLE

At the risk of appearing to be redundant, we again cite Robert Townsend, former C.E.O. of Avis Rental Cars, who put it more effectively than we ever could. In his efforts to persuade management of industry to exercise its power to eradicate racism from its ranks, he said:

This has to start with a conviction in the chief executive officer. But if he wants more than a scurry by each division to find a company black, he better follow up his bulletin as far as he is chief executive. Stamping out racism will be a process, not an act, and the chief resistance will be in the personnel office. It is results, not explanations, that count, as in other business action, and you can waste a lot of time just talking.[1]

SETTING THE TONE

Whether the issue is overt racism, or the normal problems which management must address in its day-to-day efforts to achieve its many objectives, the tone of the organization and the perception by the employees of what really matters is an extension of the personality of top management.

In the typical organization, there is a constant exploration among the employees to ascertain what is and what is not important to management. Even without formal memoranda, the discerning employee will divine what is important and what the wishes of management really are. If one accepts this premise, it follows that the problems set forth in this chapter will be addressed effectively only when it is unequivocally clear at each level of management, from senior management to first line supervisor, that top management wants these problems solved.

Fully cognizant of the crowded calendar of top management of the banking industry, we have elected to include only what we believe to be the most important of the problems which we have uncovered during our research. They include (1) the systematic exclusion of black managers from the all important communication system; (2) the marginal to poor quality of supervision of black managers; (3) the lack of clearly defined and communicated career and promotion policies and practices with respect to black managers; (4) the systematic underpayment of black female managers; and (5) last but not least, the relegation of black males to the bottom of the employment ladder.

INFORMATION AND COMMUNICATION SYSTEMS

As stated early in this document, the most significant problem faced by minority managers in the banking industry is *not knowing what is going on in the organization*. In fact, 76 percent of our respondents cited this as the most significant problem. This is a critical issue and is part and parcel of the loyalty generating process within the organization. Those who do not know what is going on do not feel that they are on the team. Persons sensing they are not on the team cannot bring the enthusiasm and energy that jobs in this highly competitive industry need.

We proceed under the assumption that adequate communication systems, both formal and informal, already exist in most banking organizations. The issue is that black and other minority managers are generally excluded from these information systems.

Perhaps the best way to assure that minorities are plugged into the communication system is for top management to give clear and unequivocal signals that minorities must be included rather than excluded. The most effective signal is for senior management to take opportunities to be seen communicating with minorities upon both planned and unplanned occasions. It is fascinating to observe how far most employees will extend themselves to emulate management.

This communication process may be facilitated by either a formal or an informal mentor system. We believe that such a system would be an exercise in futility, however, unless there was a mechanism to ascertain its results.

We are ambivalent as to which approach, the formal or the informal, would be the most effective. There are obvious constraints to the effectiveness of formal mentor systems. Such questions as these are likely to arise: How does a mentor develop a mutually viable relationship with a person whom he perceives has little or nothing in common with him? How will white employees view management's solicitous behavior toward minorities? There is, however, ample empirical evidence both within and outside the banking industry that suggests that, properly managed, a formal system can work in spite of the apparent constraints.

One practical idea that could facilitate both effective mentoring and a fluid communication process is for senior management to sponsor periodic informal receptions, cocktail parties, or similar gatherings that permit two-way conversations between senior management and minority managers. *Here, we emphasize that the problems would be exacerbated if minority managers were conspicuously singled out for special treatment by management.* Thus, we recommend that there be no all black or all minority receptions with top management. Instead, care should be given to include a cross section of first line supervisors, middle managers, and selected white peers of minorities. The obvious purpose of this type of gathering is to permit all levels of employees to observe management's interaction with the black managers. One would be amazed at the extent to which all intermediate levels of management and peers alike will seek to emulate the interaction with minorities which they observe by top management. We further emphasize that communication functions should not be superficial machinations by top management, but rather a genuine effort to communicate to each level of participant that it is desirable to include minorities on its team.

THE QUALITY OF SUPERVISION

Without question or fear of contradiction, we believe that the single most important instrument for the development or destruction of careers of minorities in the banking industry is the first line supervisor. Whether the issue is communication channels, promotion criteria, career pathing, or racism in its many forms, it is the supervisor who exerts the most direct influence.

Our research revealed that quite frequently, first line supervisors are elevated to positions of responsibility without prior training or experience in supervision. The basis of the elevation is typically, but not always, prior superior performance by the supervisor as a technician. Superior performance as a technician or specialist in a particular job may be one of the legitimate criteria for elevating an employee, but, by itself, it is totally inadequate preparation for management responsibility. The skills required to succeed in management are totally different from the skills necessary to succeed in a technical job.

Our research also revealed that supervisors who are the least skilled in management techniques are also the most insecure. They then inflict their insecurity upon their employees in ways that tend to stifle development, block communication channels, and inhibit productivity.

We, therefore, would recommend first that a supervisor should be required to take not only a crash course in supervision and management before he is allowed to assume his new responsibilities, but also, he should be required to take management seminars on a systematic and intermittent basis for an indeterminate period until his empirical management results suggest that he has mastered sound management techniques.

To ascertain the degree to which he has mastered these techniques, the personnel department should be empowered to take employee opinion surveys within his department at three to six month intervals during this first year, and annually thereafter. These surveys should contain all of the basic questions that suggest whether or not the supervisor is a good manager. They should be charted over time to ascertain the degree of improvement in his management skills. The survey instruments should be anonymous so as to encourage candor among the employees.

Secondly, there should be a system of employee redress that would prevent a tyrannical supervisor from crushing the career of a good employee on arbitrary grounds. We encountered numerous instances of banks that allowed their first line supervisors to run roughshod over his employees even when the supervisor was known to be wrong. A policy that officially permits an aggrieved employee to pursue redress without fear of retribution would ameliorate this problem.

Such a system was the hallmark of the I.B.M. human resource development system from its early inception. Is it any wonder that no one in its industry can challenge "Big Blue's" dominance? It continues to recruit, train, develop, and retain the best people in the industry. The evidence is clear and unequivocal that its people are its most important products. It is no accident.

Finally, we recommend that, like many well-run organizations, the banking industry considers adopting a human resource development system that requires a supervisor to not only train that person's replacement, but also to show how he has brought along each person in his organization with respect to future development. Such an evaluation criterion should be given sufficient weight that it would motivate the supervisor to take the responsibility seriously. Such a responsibility should be an integral part of the bank's accountability management system, which it uses to evaluate and reward/punish managers in profit, cost, or other responsibility centers. This would contribute to the solution of the tyrannical supervisor who routinely crushes good employees because of his insecurities. Such a system could not help but strengthen the most important asset of a bank, its human resources.

CAREER GUIDANCE AND PROMOTION
POLICIES AND PRACTICES

Our respondents repeatedly indicated that they frequently encountered difficulties in their attempts to solicit career guidance from their supervisors. Even when there were formal review processes, the reviews were performed perfunctorily, even grudgingly. We encountered bankers who virtually had to confront their supervisor in order to get an evaluation. Others who were less aggressive worked for extended periods of time without a formal evaluation that could be placed in their personnel file. On the other hand, many of our respondents revealed that it was obvious their white peers received constant feedback regarding their performance as well as counsel regarding their career options.

This dual treatment of the bank's employees can only serve to stifle the minority employees at the expense of loyalty and productivity.

There are obviously many reasons that supervisors could offer as excuses for not developing and bringing black professionals along in the bank's manpower development system. As Townsend said, however, "If management is serious, excuses will not be acceptable for failure to get desired results regarding this issue."

If the bank feels its current personnel cannot effectively address the problem of underutilization of black professionals, it may wish to bring in consultants who, by training and experience, could assist the bank in its efforts to bridge the communication gap between its minority professionals and the bank management hierarchy. Many non-financial corporations already take this approach.

BLACK WOMEN UNDERPAID AND UNDERUTILIZED

The evidence is striking and conclusive that black females are being underpaid by the industry. This underpayment is in relationship to black males, as our research reveals, but we suspect this practice would be equally true, if not more pronounced, with respect to white males and females, an issue beyond the scope of our research. This underpayment prevails whether the comparative criterion is age, education, tenure in the industry, or tenure in the current employer bank.

There is absolutely no function in the banking industry that black women cannot master in the same degree as other bank employees, just as there are no functions that white women cannot master, given the opportunity. The practice of underpaying black women under all conditions suggests that the industry is opting for black women over black men as a means of saving money. It is equally plausible, however, that the industry might opt for black women over black men even if it had to equate the salaries of black women with those of black men.

Whatever the motivation for this employment and salary behavior on the part of the industry, the practice adversely affects the earning power of black women while at the same time it selects out black men. We recommend therefore that this practice be carefully evaluated and ameliorated by top management of the banking industry, if not for moral and productivity reasons, then for legal reasons.

INDUSTRY ESCHEWS BLACK MEN

Our final recommendation has to do with the situation in which the banking industry has systematically eschewed or selected out black male managers during the last seven years. The evidence shows that the industry is choosing women over black men. White women to a larger extent, but also black women have been hired and retained at greater rates than black men.

E.E.O.C. statistics show that of the 268,729 management jobs created in the banking industry between 1966 and 1981, 43 percent have been awarded to white women, 4 percent have been awarded to black women and 3.5 percent have been awarded to black men. The percentage of white men at the management level dropped from 87 to 54 percent during this period. Nevertheless, this still leaves white males as the dominant labor sector of the banking industry at the management level. By contrast, black men were kept out of the industry at the management level prior to 1960. After about five years of marginal improvement, however, black men have been relegated to the numerical bottom of the management ladder.

This is true in spite of the fact that black males in the industry have achieved educational levels superior to black females. Furthermore, while we did not research it, we would not be surprised if objective evidence showed that black males also exceed the educational level of white females in the banking industry.

It is conceivable that the fact that black female college graduates have in recent years outnumbered black male college graduates could have influenced the selection process. In this regard, however, the industry hired more white women than white men, in spite of the fact that there were significantly more white men in the labor force than white women. Thus, the large pool of white men did not stop the industry from seeking out those white women managers it wanted.

Similarly, black men and women had about the same relative percentage participation in the labor force. Nonetheless, the industry chose the black female. It is clear, therefore, that the industry did not use either education or labor supply availability as its selection criteria for black males or females.

We also discovered widespread evidence of the industry's propensity to discourage the hiring of aggressive black males, no matter how well educated, polished, or articulate. Our personal interviewees, both male and female, told us that while these characteristics are highly valued in the white male, the black male with these characteristics will either not be hired, or if he is employed, is likely to leave out of frustration, or be fired. Those black males who have these characteristics and who survive generally live under a great deal of internal stress in their effort to submerge their true personalities.

Although we are not medical doctors, we observed some very sharp black males who obviously were suffering in their efforts to live with themselves and their jobs. Many talked frankly while others attempted to hide their frustrations.

NEEDED: TOP MANAGEMENT COMMITMENT

We believe this situation to be a scandal of enormous proportions for the banking industry, and that there is no rational reason for the industry to select women, white or black, over black male managers.

We further recommend that if this trend has not previously come to the attention of top management, now that it is a documented fact, the industry should without delay initiate strategies to recruit, train, and develop black males, utilizing the same criteria that it uses for its white males. At the risk of being redundant, we repeat that the most critical factors in the ultimate success of such a program are (1) the believability of the commitment of top management, (2) the quality of first line supervisors and middle managers, and (3) an objective measurement system of the performance and accountability of these managers, with respect to this issue.

In conclusion, this and future research will demonstrate, in our opinion, that black and other minorities function in a less than hospitable environment as they seek careers in the banking industry. They are consciously seeking the ear of top management to ameliorate these problems. It just may be in the self-interest of top management to listen. Only history can answer this question, however.

NOTE

1. Robert Townsend, *Up the Organization* (New York: Alfred Knopf, 1970), p. 161.

APPENDIX

THE URBAN BANKERS JOB AND
CAREER DYNAMICS QUESTIONNAIRE

NOTE: (1) The scale from one to five conveys the following meaning: 1 — Excellent to true; 2 — is above average; 4 — is below average and 5 — is poor or false.

NOTE: (2) Return this form unsigned to: NAUB, 915 15th Street, NW, Suite 600 Washington, D.C. 20005

	1	2	3	4	5	

I. INDUSTRY ASSESSMENT

1. I believe that the Banking Industry affords more and varied opportunities for minority Americans than do most.   ( ) ( ) ( ) ( ) ( )   (4)

2. Minority Americans are currently afforded the same opportunities in the Banking Industry as white Americans.   ( ) ( ) ( ) ( ) ( )   (5)

II. INSTITUTIONAL RELATIONSHIPS

1. This company is a good place to work.   ( ) ( ) ( ) ( ) ( )   (6)
2. I am given a chance to do things I do best.   ( ) ( ) ( ) ( ) ( )   (7)
3. I believe I can achieve my career goals in this institution.   ( ) ( ) ( ) ( ) ( )   (8)
4. I would leave the bank if something better comes along.   ( ) ( ) ( ) ( ) ( )   (9)

                                                    1   2   3   4   5

5. My bank is just as vigorously seeking
minorities today as they were five years
ago.   ( ) ( ) ( ) ( ) ( ) (10)
6. PLEASE RANK the three (3) most impor-
tant problems minorities face in the Banking Industry. (With one being the most
important)
( ) 1. racism   (11-13)
( ) 2. not knowing what's going on in
the organization (not in network)
( ) 3. not being given a chance to learn
new jobs
( ) 4. poor pay
( ) 5. inability to get a mentor
( ) 6. other _____
7. I would rate the promotion criteria cited
below as follows:
A. Technical knowledge   ( ) ( ) ( ) ( ) ( ) (14)
B. Communication skills   ( ) ( ) ( ) ( ) ( ) (15)
(a) oral   ( ) ( ) ( ) ( ) ( ) (16)
(b) written   ( ) ( ) ( ) ( ) ( ) (17)
C. Personality   ( ) ( ) ( ) ( ) ( ) (18)
D. Who do you know (office politics)   ( ) ( ) ( ) ( ) ( ) (19)
E. Hard work   ( ) ( ) ( ) ( ) ( ) (20)
F. Appearance   ( ) ( ) ( ) ( ) ( ) (21)
G. Education (in general)   ( ) ( ) ( ) ( ) ( ) (22)
(a) the school you came from   ( ) ( ) ( ) ( ) ( ) (23)
(b) an M.B.A.   ( ) ( ) ( ) ( ) ( ) (24)

III.   SUPERVISOR RELATIONSHIP
1. My supervisor is competent in doing
his/her job.   ( ) ( ) ( ) ( ) ( ) (25)
2. My responsibilities are clearly defined.   ( ) ( ) ( ) ( ) ( ) (26)
3. My supervisor is concerned about my
welfare.   ( ) ( ) ( ) ( ) ( ) (27)
4. My supervisor helps prepare me for the
next step on the career ladder.   ( ) ( ) ( ) ( ) ( ) (28)
5. My supervisor gives me credit for my
ideas rather than take credit for himself/
herself.   ( ) ( ) ( ) ( ) ( ) (29)
6. My supervisor invites me to social func-
tions outside the bank.   ( ) ( ) ( ) ( ) ( ) (30)

1 2 3 4 5

7. My performance evaluations are fair and
   objective.   ( ) ( ) ( ) ( ) ( ) (31)

IV.   FINANCIAL REWARDS
   1. My salary is comparable to others doing
      similar work and with similar qualifica-
      tions.   ( ) ( ) ( ) ( ) ( ) (32)
   2. I feel secure on my job.   ( ) ( ) ( ) ( ) ( ) (33)
   3. My salary currently is (check one)
                              (thousands)
      ( ) below $25   ( ) $45–49   ( ) $70 & above
      ( ) $25–29   ( ) 50–59
      ( ) 30–44   ( ) 60–69   (34)

V.   PROMOTION DYNAMICS
   1. Promotions are handled fair in this bank. ( ) ( ) ( ) ( ) ( ) (35)
   2. My chances for promotion are good.   ( ) ( ) ( ) ( ) ( ) (36)
   3. Minority Americans have the same chance
      for promotion as white Americans.   ( ) ( ) ( ) ( ) ( ) (37)
   4. The labor sectors listed below are cur-
      rently being hired and promoted in the
      following rank order in my bank. (Please
      rank from 1 to 4)   (38)
      ( ) white men   ( ) white women
      ( ) black men   ( ) black women
   5. My perception is that persons who get
      rapid promotions have mentors.   ( ) ( ) ( ) ( ) ( ) (42)
   6. I have a mentor.   ( ) ( ) ( ) ( ) ( ) (43)
   7. Minority Americans *generally* do not
      have mentors.   ( ) ( ) ( ) ( ) ( ) (44)

VI.   PEER RELATIONSHIPS
   1. The people I work with are genuinely
      friendly.   ( ) ( ) ( ) ( ) ( ) (45)
   2. The people I work with pitch in to help
      me when they perceive that I need it.   ( ) ( ) ( ) ( ) ( ) (46)
   3. My peers often invite me to coffee or
      lunch.   ( ) ( ) ( ) ( ) ( ) (47)
   4. My peers often invite me to social
      functions outside the bank.   ( ) ( ) ( ) ( ) ( ) (48)

VII.   TENURE, FUNCTION, RANK
  1. I have been in the banking industry
     (Check one)
     ( ) Below 5 years   ( ) 10–14   (49-52)
     ( ) 5–9   ( ) 15 & above
  2. I have been with my current bank:
     (Check one)
     ( ) Below 5 years   ( ) 10–14   (53-56)
     ( ) 5–9   ( ) 15 & above
  3. My function is: (Check one)
     ( ) 1) Commercial lending   ( ) Investment   (57)
     ( ) 2) Retail Lending   ( ) Operations (any)
                                  ( ) Other
  4. My title now is:
     ( ) Banking officer or below ( ) Sr. V.P.   (58)
     ( ) Assistant V.P.   ( ) Other
     ( ) V.P.

VIII. EDUCATION
  The highest education level I have attained
  is: (Check one)
     ( ) high school   ( ) M.B.A.   (59)
     ( ) some college   ( ) other masters
     ( ) bachelor's degree   ( ) above masters

IX.   AGE RANK
     ( ) under 25 years   ( ) 35–39   (60)
     ( ) 25–29   ( ) 40–45
     ( ) 30–34   ( ) above 45

X.   SIZE OF BANK (Assets)
     ( ) under $1 billion   (61)
     ( ) $1 billion
     ( ) $5 billion to 14.9
     ( ) $15 billion to 24.9
     ( ) $25 billion and above

XI.   SEX   ( ) Male   (62)
             ( ) Female

BIBLIOGRAPHY

Alderter, C. P., Alderter, C. J., Tucker, L., and R. Tucker. "Diagnosing Race Relations in Management." *Journal of Applied Behavioral Science* 16 (April-May-June 1980): 135-36.

Alexander, Rodney. *The Negro in the Banking Industry*. New York: Dunellen, 1973.

Alexis, Marcus. "A Theory of Labor Market Discrimination with Interdependent Utilities." *American Economic Association Proceedings and Papers* 63 (May 1973).

America, R. F. and B. E. Anderson. "Must Black Executives Be Superstars?" *Wharton Magazine* 3 (Spring 1979): 44-48.

Argyris, Chris. *Understanding Organizational Behavior*. Homewood, Ill.: Dorsey Press, 1960.

——. *Personality and Organization: The System and the Individuals*. New York: Harper and Row Publishers, 1957.

——. "Banking on a Career, with Education Plus Experience." *American Banking Association Banking Journal* 72 (November 1980): 125.

Bartolome, Fernando and Evans, Paul A. Lee. "Must Success Cost So Much?" *Harvard Business Review* 58, No. 2 (March-April 1980): 137-48.

Becker, Gary. *Economics of Discrimination*. Chicago: University of Chicago Press, 1971.

Benson, C. A. "The Question of Mobility in Career Development for Black Professionals." *Personnel Journal* 54 (May 1975): 40-43.

Benson, Herbert. "Your Innate Asset for Combating Stress." *Harvard Business Review* 52 (July-August 1974).

Benson, Herbert and Allen, Robert L. "How Much Stress Is Too Much?" *Harvard Business Review* 58.

Berger, Chester. *Survival in the Executive Jungle*. New York: Macmillan, 1964.

Bowman, Gorda W. "What Helps or Harms Promotability." In Paths Toward Personal Progress. *Harvard Business Review* 60 (1982): 94.

Brimmer, Andrew F. "The Patience Factor: Management Careers in Corporate Enterprise." *Black Enterprise* 13 (September 1982): 30.

Burris, Beverly H. *No Room at the Top: Underemployment and Alienation in the Corporation*. New York: Praeger Publishers, 1983.

Carter, Hodding III. "The U.S. Has Yet to Expunge the Stain of Racism." *Wall Street Journal* 26 (April 1984): 29.

Collins, G. C. and Patricia Scott. "Everyone Who Makes It Has a Mentor." *Harvard Business Review* 56 (July-August 1978): 135.

Cooper, Alfred M. *How to Supervise People*. New York: McGraw-Hill Books, 1958.

Darrity, William, Jr. "The Human Capital Approach to Black/White Earnings Inequality: Some Unsettled Questions." *Journal of Human Resources* 17 (Winter 1982).

Datcher, Linda, Malveany, Julianne, and Phyllis Wallace. *Black Women in the Labor Force*. Cambridge, Mass.: Institute of Technology, 1980.

Davis, George and Glegg Watson. *Black Life in Corporate America*. Garden City, New York: Anchor Press, 1982.

Dickens, Floyd, Jr. and Jacqueline B. Dickens. "Style of Black Management." *Supervisory Management* 27 (January 1982): 8-11.

_____ . *Black Managers: Making It in the Corporate World*. The American Management Association, 1982.

Diggory, James C. "Status, Ability and Self Esteem." *Frontier of Management Psychology*, edited by John C. Diggory. New York: Harper and Row, 1964.

Doeringer, Peter and Piore, Michael. *Internal Labor Markets and Manpower Analysis*. Lexington, Mass.: D.C. Heath and Co., 1971.

Dorfman, Ron. "A Black Bank: The Promised Land Was Chicago First National." *Business and Society Review* (Spring 1976): 43-44.

Erickson, R. J. "The Changing Workplace and Workforce." *Training and Development Journal* 34 (January 1980): 62-65.

Ewing, David B. "Tension Can Be an Asset." *Harvard Business Review* 42, No. 5 (September-October 1964): 71-78.

Fernandez, John P. *Racism and Sexism in Corporate Life.* Lexington, Mass.: Lexington Books, 1981.

_____. *Black Managers in White Corporations.* New York: Wiley, 1975.

Ford, D. L., Jr. and D. S. Beghot. "Correlates of Job Stress and Job Satisfaction for Minority Professionals in Organizations: An Examination of Personal and Organizational Factors." *Group and Organization Studies* 3 (March 1978: 30-41.

Freeman, Richard B. "Decline of Labor Market Discrimination." *American Economic Association Proceedings and Papers* 64 (May 1973a).

_____. "Labor Market for Black Americans, 1948-72." Okum, Arthur M. and Perry, George L., eds. *Brookings Papers in Economic Activity* 1973b.

Friedman, Milton. *Capitalism and Freedom.* Chicago: University of Chicago Press, 1962.

Gabarro, John G. and John P. Ketter. "Managing Your Boss." *Harvard Business Review* 58 (January-February 1980): 94-95.

Greenbergor, Robert S. "Up the Ladder: Many Black Managers Hope to Enter the Ranks of Top Management: But Despite Much Optimism, the Big Test Lies Ahead; Subtle Racism Lingers on, Trying to be 'Team Player'." *Wall Street Journal* 104 (June 15, 1981): 1.

Hayes, Kathleen C. "If Minorities Quit, Spirit of Affirmative Action Isn't Being Met." *ABA Banking Journal* 74 (December 1984): 14.

Herbert, Therdone T. *Organizational Behavior, Readings and Cases.* New York: Macmillan Publishing Co., Inc., 1976.

"How a Social Conscience Shapes Banking." *Business Week*, September 15, 1973, pp. 140-41.

Jordan, I. L. and E. C. Jordan. "Affirmative Action and the Black Manager." *Personnel Journal* 60 (February 1983): 155-57.

Johnson, J. H. "Failure is a Word I Don't Accept." *Harvard Business Review* 54 (March-April 1976): 79-88.

"Judge Holds Up Chemical Accord with Black Employees in Bias Suit." *American Banker* 146 (April 1981): 3.

Katz, Daniel and Robert Kahn. *The Social Psychology of Organizations*. New York: John Wiley and Sons, 1966.

Kiechell, Walter III. "The Care and Feeding of Contacts." *Fortune* (February 8, 1982): 119.

Kovak, Kenneth. "What People Want from Their Work." *Advance Management Journal* 45 (Spring 1980): 56.

Lawrence, Paul R. *Organizational Behavior and Administration Cases, Concepts, and Research Findings*. Homewood, Ill.: Richard D. Irwin, 1965.

Lea, Daniel and Zandy B. Leibowitz. "Mentor: Would You Know One If You Saw One." *Supervisory Management* 15 (April 1983): 34.

Levinson, Harry. *Emotional Health: In the World of Work*. rev. ed. New York: Harper and Row, 1964.

_____. "Psychological Man." *Harvard Business Review* 56 (January-February 1978): 120-24.

_____. "On Executive Suicide." *Harvard Business Review* (July-August 1975): 118-22.

_____. "What Killed Bob Lyons?" *Harvard Business Review* 59, No. 2 (March-April 1981): 144-62.

Lombardo, Michael M. and Morgan, V. McCall, Jr. "The Intolerable Boss." *Psychology Today* 18 (January 1984): 44-47.

Maccoby, Michael. *The Gamesman*. New York: Simon and Schuster, 1970.

Malveaux, Juliane M. *Women in the Workplace*. Boston: Augurn House Publishing, 1982.

Marshall, Ray. "Black Employment in the South." In Phyllis A. Wallace and Annette M. Lamond, *Women, Common Minorities, and Employment Discrimination*. Cambridge, Mass.: MIT, 1977.

Matthews, Gordon. "Chemical Settles Suit by Black Staff: Will Provide $400,000, Established Ombudsman." *American Banker* 146 (March 3, 1981): 12.

Menninger, Karl A. *Man Against Himself*. New York: Harcourt Brace Jovanovich, 1938.

Milbourn, G., Jr. and R. Cuba. "What Blacks Want From Their Jobs — and What They Get." *Sam Advanced Management Journal* 45 (Autumn 1980): 50-60.

Mosko, Andrew M. *1983 BAI Bank Officer Cash Compensation Survey*. Rolling Meadows, Ill.: Bank Administration Institute, 1983.

Norton, Eleanor Holmes. "Struggle for the Executive Suite — Black vs. White Women." *Black Enterprise* 11 (September 1980): 24.

Peters, Ruanne K. and Herbert Benson. "Time Out from Tension." *Harvard Business Review* 53 (July-August 1975): 118-22.

Raelin, Joseph A. *The Salaried Professional — How to Make the Most of Your Career*. New York: Praeger Publishers, 1984.

Ringer, Richard. "Push Targets Banking Industry for Aid Pledge to Black Communities." *American Banker* (August 13, 1982): 3(2).

Roach, Gerald R. "Much Ado About Mentors." *Harvard Business Review* (January-February 1979): 16.

Rubenstein, James. "Harris Vows to Fight Award of $12.1 Million Back Pay in Bias Ruling: Says It Will Not Yield to Government 'Blackmail' by Settling Now." *American Banker* 146 (March 19, 1982): 3(2).

Rumberger, Russell W. *Overeducation in the U.S. Labor Market*. New York: Praeger Publishers, 1981.

Schatzman, D. "Why Corporations Are Having Trouble Retaining Competent Black Professionals." *Vital Speeches* 45 (August 15, 1979): 664-66.

Simmons, Judy. "Pinstripes and Other Attitudes." *Black Enterprise* 9 (January 1979): 31-34.

Sowell, Thomas. *Markets and Minorities*. New York: Basic Books, 1981.

Stein, Edgar H. *Career Dynamics: Matching Individual and Organizational Needs*. Reading, Mass.: Addison-Wesley, 1978.

Swinton, David. "Racial Inequality in the New South." *Adherent* 10 (Fall 1983).

_____. "Orthodox and Systematic Explanations for Unemployment and Racial Inequality." *The Reviews of Black Political Economy* 12 (Spring 1983).

Theibolt, Armand J. *The Negro in the Banking Industry*. Philadelphia: University of Pennsylvania Press, 1970.

Thurow, Lester. *Generating Inequality: Mechanisms of Distribution in the U.S. Economy*. New York: Basic Books, Inc., 1975.

"U.S. Invest- Or a Stern Banker." *Tomorrow's Banker* 87 (February 23, 1976): 5-6.

Townsend, Robert. *Up the Organization*. New York: Knopf, 1970.

Van Fleet, James K. *Guide to Managing People — How to Control People through Dynamic Leadership and Supervision*. West Nyack, N.Y.: Parker Publisher, 1968.

Weiler, Nichols. *Reality and Career Planning*. Reading, Mass.: Addison-Wesley, 1977.

Work, J. W. "Management Blacks and the Internal Labor Market: Responses to a Questionnaire." *Human Resources Management* (Fall 1980): 27-31.

Yerkes, Robert M. and Dodson, John D. "The Relation of Strength of Stimulus to Rapidity of Habit-Formation." *Journal of Comparative Neurology and Psychology* (1908): 459.

ABOUT THE AUTHORS

EDWARD D. IRONS is a professor and a financial and management consultant. He has been an entrepreneur and executive in the banking and venture capital industries. He was principal organizer and first president of Riverside National Bank, Houston, Texas, the first national bank charter to be granted to black Americans in the 40 years prior to its opening; later, he became president of the New York Urban Coalition Venture Capital Corporation, New York City. In addition, he served as Chief of the Investment Survey Division of the Agency for International Development, U.S. Department of State during the Kennedy and Johnson era.

During his 20 years as an educator, he has taught at several universities, including Texas Southern University, Howard University, The University of Richmond, and Atlanta University Center, where since 1971, he has served as the Mills B. Lane Professor of Banking and Finance, Atlanta University Center, Atlanta, Georgia.

He has published widely in banking and financial journals. He received a BS from Central State University, a Master's Degree from the University of Minnesota, and a DBA in Finance from Harvard University Graduate School of Business. He was a Ford Foundation Post Doctoral Fellow at the University of Michigan, Survey Research Center.

He is a former chairman, and a current director of the National Economic Association, a member of the Financial Executive Institute, and a director of Lincoln National Life Insurance Corporation.

GILBERT MOORE is professor of Economics at Morehouse College. Previous academic appointments include Distinguished Professor of Labor Economics at Benedic College and professorships at Harvard, the University of Texas/Dallas, and the Massachusetts Institute of Technology. Dr. Moore's publications include research monographs on labor market discrimination and the employment impacts of federal labor market policy. Dr. Moore received his BA degree from Stanford University, and his MA and Ph.D. degrees from Princeton University. He is the father of two children.